WHAT YOUR COLLEAGUES ARE

"Leave it to Sara Holbrook and Michael Salinger to come up with a resource that allows kids to be the diverse group of individuals they can and want to be—and at the same time paves a route for them to meet the Common Core Standards. . . . I really wish I had written this resource. Having read it, it is tough not to be jealous."

—STEPHANIE HARVEY, Coauthor of *Strategies That Work*, Second Edition

"High-Impact Writing Clinics is a unique, practical, clever, and just-right-for-the-times resource. Poetry *is* an integral part of the Common Core Standards. And just in time, here comes a truly easy-to-use resource, with all the connections made, lessons provided, ready-to-use slides, and texts included. If you can turn on PowerPoint, you can teach these lessons!"

—HARVEY "SMOKEY" DANIELS, Coauthor of *The Best-Kept Teaching Secret*

"Is poetry relevant in this era of Common Core? Absolutely! Anyone who doubts this needs to pick up this remarkable book by Sara Holbrook and Michael Salinger, who show how poetry is not only relevant but an engaging way for students to meet these rigorous standards. . . . Sara and Michael show students (and their teachers) the power of imagination and observation, even as they read closely and work to meet the standards."

—STEVI QUATE, Independent Consultant and Staff Developer, Public Education & Business Coalition (PEBC)

"I highly recommend this resource for all teachers. In addition to showing how each lesson addresses the Common Core State Standards, Sara and Michael demystify poetry writing for students of all ages. This book also includes poems that exemplify, extend, and reinforce each lesson. Using *High-Impact Writing Clinics* is like having Sara and Michael as enthusiastic co-teachers in your own classroom."

—BEVERLY ANN CHIN, PhD, Director, English Teaching Program, University of Montana

"As I read *High-Impact Writing Clinics,* I felt as though I had been transported back to my own classroom with two amazing poets in residence. Sara Holbrook and Michael Salinger give teachers and writers the tools to make the world stand still so we can capture a moment in words. The lessons and original poems bring writers to the sights and sounds that are at the heart of a real writing workshop."

—JANET ALLEN, Author of *Plugged Into Reading*

DVD
INCLUDED!

HIGH-IMPACT
WRITING
CLINICS

20 Projectable Lessons for
Building Literacy Across Content Areas

SARA HOLBROOK
MICHAEL SALINGER

Foreword by
STEPHANIE HARVEY

CORWIN
A SAGE Company

FOR INFORMATION:

Corwin
A SAGE Company
2455 Teller Road
Thousand Oaks, California 91320
(800) 233-9936
www.corwin.com

SAGE Publications Ltd.
1 Oliver's Yard
55 City Road
London EC1Y 1SP
United Kingdom

SAGE Publications India Pvt. Ltd.
B 1/I 1 Mohan Cooperative Industrial Area
Mathura Road, New Delhi 110 044
India

SAGE Publications Asia-Pacific Pte. Ltd.
3 Church Street
#10-04 Samsung Hub
Singapore 049483

Publisher: Lisa Luedeke
Development Editor: Julie Nemer
Editorial Assistant: Francesca Dutra Africano
Production Editor: Melanie Birdsall
Copy Editor: Sarah J. Duffy
Typesetter: C&M Digitals (P) Ltd.
Proofreader: Theresa Kay
Indexer: Karen Wiley
Cover Designer: Gail Buschman

Printed in the United States of America

Library of Congress Cataloging-in-Publication Data

Holbrook, Sara.

High-impact writing clinics : 20 projectable lessons for building literacy across content areas / Sara Holbrook, Michael Salinger.

pages cm
Includes index.

ISBN 978-1-4522-8686-0 (pbk.)

1. English language—Composition and exercises. 2. Creative writing—Study and teaching. I. Salinger, Michael. II. Title.

PE1404.H635 2013
808.'04207—dc23   2013015842

This book is printed on acid-free paper.

SUSTAINABLE FORESTRY INITIATIVE
Certified Chain of Custody
Promoting Sustainable Forestry
www.sfiprogram.org
SFI-01268
SFI label applies to text stock

13 14 15 16 17 10 9 8 7 6 5 4 3 2 1

Contents

At-a-Glance Clinic Descriptions

Clinics with potential for cross curricular use are noted as such in the list below.

Clinic	Purpose	Content Areas
Clinic 1. Objective Versus Subjective	Clinic 1 is designed to help students **differentiate between fact and opinion.** Opinion words (aka subjective terms) are not effective when writing fiction, literary nonfiction, or science reports. Good writers use **evidence** to support opinions. **Preface to the writing of persuasive and informational text.**	Language Arts, Science, Social Studies
Clinic 2. The List Poem	Clinic 2 is designed to further help students **differentiate between fact and opinion.** Students gather specifics and form a word list to describe a person, place, or thing, prioritizing information gathered from sources. **Demonstrates the importance of evaluating and integrating pertinent details when writing explanatory texts.**	Science, Language Arts, Social Studies
Clinic 3. The Summary Poem	Clinic 3 is designed to help students master simple narrative structure, which they use to summarize an event or a piece of text. Students then cull their own writing, identifying the most important words. In doing so, students practice **determining a central idea and summarize their observations in a clear and coherent summary.**	Language Arts, Social Studies, Science
Clinic 4. The Found Poem	Clinic 4 leads students to compose two poems, one based on a setting and one based on a piece of text. In the first part, students gather details from a place. In Part 2, students closely analyze a piece of text and identify the most important words. **Leads to a closer eye for detail and closer reading of text.**	Language Arts, Social Studies, Science
Clinic 5. Feelings Made Visual	Clinic 5 leads students to **closely read and analyze the structure of a poem.** Students then convey what they have experienced, imagined, thought, and felt in **concrete terms that communicate meaning to their audience.**	Language Arts, Science
Clinic 6. Couplets on the Brain	Clinic 6 helps students understand and explain how a series of stanzas fits together, and furthers their understanding of a structure that **uses rhyming couplets. Students learn the power of couplets to communicate information.**	Language Arts, Science, Math
Clinic 7. No Longer the Same	Clinic 7 is designed in two parts. In Part 1, students follow a pattern to compare and contrast events in their own lives that demonstrate change. In Part 2, through **research of multiple sources,** students use the same pattern to demonstrate their content learning and write an informational poem evidencing change, **comparing what was to what is.**	Language Arts, Science, Social Studies
Clinic 8. The Questioning Poem	Clinic 8 leads students to look at subject matter, **formulate questions,** and then collaborate in small groups, **prioritizing** their **questions** into a single piece of text.	Language Arts, Science, Social Studies
Clinic 9. Refrain: Come Again?	Clinic 9 leads students to **determine two main ideas about a topic (or text) and use those in a piece of writing that summarizes,** utilizing a refrain. Additionally, they discuss the text elements of repetition and refrain.	Science, Language Arts, Social Studies

Clinic	Purpose	Content Areas
Clinic 10. Personification	Clinic 10 helps students develop an understanding of figurative language including personification, similes, synonyms, and antonyms. Students **revise their work by eliminating excess words.** By personifying an emotion, **students use well-chosen details to create figurative meaning.**	Language Arts, Science
Clinic 11. Point of View	Clinic 11 helps develop students' understanding of voice as they write from a point of view other than their own. Writing from the point of view of an object or word, **students will use multiple sources to research their poems and employ figurative language to convey an idea.**	Language Arts, Math, Science, Social Studies
Clinic 12. Word Definition Poems	Clinic 12 leads students to consult reference materials (both print and digital) to find pronunciation and to determine or clarify the precise meaning of a content area vocabulary word. Writing a word definition poem will help them to **develop a nuanced understanding of the word, including synonyms and antonyms.**	Language Arts, Math, Science, Social Studies
Clinic 13. Weighting the Evidence	Clinic 13 is designed in two parts. In Part 1, students prioritize observations about a person, place, or thing while writing a text using percentages. In Part 2, they write a poem using measurement terms. In both parts, **students determine the relative importance of information and details as they effectively select them and organize their poem.**	Language Arts, Math, Science, Social Studies (economics)
Clinic 14. The Prepositional Phrase Poem	Clinic 14 first asks students to analyze the use of prepositional phrases and how they are used in a piece of text to convey setting and motion. Through this, they come to understand that a prepositional phrase modifies a noun or a verb. **Students demonstrate their understanding of prepositional phrases through their writing.**	Language Arts, Social Studies, Science, Math (calculus)
Clinic 15. Simile for Me	Clinic 15 provides students with a deeper understanding of figurative language as they first analyze a poem and then compose a poem that describes themselves using similes. As they incorporate similes into their writing, **students demonstrate their knowledge of figurative language.**	Language Arts, Social Studies
Clinic 16. Metaphor Mentor Text	Clinic 16 has two parts. Part 1 leads students to closer reading as they carefully analyze a poem that incorporates metaphor; they then utilize that poem as mentor text for their own composition. In Part 2, students describe one thing in terms of another, beginning with a list of Topography terms. This **strengthens students' understanding of the nuanced meanings of content area words.**	Language Arts, Social Studies, Science
Clinic 17. Exquisite Metaphors	Clinic 17 helps students find meaning in metaphors using the surrealistic parlor game Exquisite Corpse. Students utilize parts of speech to create a random sentence and ascribe meaning to it through thinking and writing. First, they **analyze and compare two pieces of writing** using this method and then they **create a metaphorical comparison of their own.**	Language Arts
Clinic 18. The Extended Metaphor	Clinic 18 helps students describe an event utilizing metaphor. This is the most sophisticated of all of the clinics. **Students use their knowledge of details, sequencing, prioritizing, conventions, and figurative language to describe a personal conflict utilizing an extended metaphor.**	Language Arts
Clinic 19. Revision Up Close	Clinic 19 provides a baker's dozen (13) of editing tips that students may use to revise their own work and to revise collaboratively with others. This is not intended to be taught as one lesson, but rather to be reviewed one or two tips at a time. You may wish to duplicate the handout so that students can keep a copy for easy reference. **Clinic reinforces language lessons by asking students to focus on specific aspects of revision.**	Language Arts, Social Studies (current and past events)
Clinic 20. Speaking Out	Clinic 20 provides **tips for public speaking,** which may be utilized throughout all the clinics.	Language Arts, Social Studies

Foreword

In a recent Ted Talk, *Education's Death Valley*, international arts and education guru Sir Ken Robinson lays out three principles that he deems crucial for the mind to flourish: diversity, curiosity, and creativity. He begins by stating that human beings are naturally different and diverse. He goes on to say that curiosity is the engine of learning, and adds that human life is inherently creative. He shares that children are best served with a broad curriculum that celebrates a wide variety of talents, not just a small, limited range of them. He emphasizes the power of the arts in human development. He notes, however, that recent American education has largely ignored these three principles, and he laments the sky-rocketing dropout rate under a law ironically titled No Child Left Behind (NCLB). The truth is, the more we standardize education, the more children we leave behind. The more we stress conformity, the more likely it is that kids will leave school unfulfilled. We need to inspire them to be diverse, flexible, creative thinkers who burst with curiosity, and explore, learn, and achieve at the highest levels.

But what's a teacher to do in this era of common standards? Teachers live in the real world and they teach in the world of standardized education. Under NCLB, many kids read from basals where all eyes in the class gaze at the same page. Their book choices are often limited to whole class novels. And they spend countless hours bubbling answers in test prep packets. Teachers know only too well how schools emphasize uniformity. And yet they know from where Sir Ken speaks. I have never met a teacher who didn't understand the importance of diversity, curiosity, and creativity. Teachers brim with delight when one of their kids does something unexpected—paints an abstract image, crafts a clever poem, designs a robotic machine, or even blurts out distaste for mystery meat in the lunchroom. So how can teachers reconcile these crucial principles with common standards so that our schools do not lapse into black holes of boredom and low achievement?

Enter Sara Holbrook and Michael Salinger. Leave it to these wildly curious and creative poets to come up with a resource that allows kids to be the diverse group of individuals they can and want to be—and at the same time paves a route for them to meet the Common Core State Standards.

High-Impact Writing Clinics seriously rocks! Sara and Michael understand that the most direct route to learning is engagement and the most direct route to engagement is fun. And fun is contagious. As I watched Sara and Michael teach one of these clinics, the enjoyment of everyone in the room, teachers and children alike, was palpable.

This power-packed resource with lesson plans, PowerPoints, compelling images, and original poetry is at its core engaging and entertaining. *High-Impact Writing Clinics* is steeped in best practices for developing writing and communication skills, but the fact that it is laced with FUN throughout sets it apart.

They call these writing exercises clinics, derived from the athletic notion of golf or tennis clinics, where you work on a part of your game, keep developing it, and use what you have learned to improve. But these writing clinics are more than lessons. They are designed for flexibility. You can do them just as they are designed, and you can also adopt and adapt them to support your current curriculum goals and to build writing capacity and strengthen kids' communication skills in every content area.

High-Impact Writing Clinics contains twenty clinics. Each clinic begins with the rationale for the lesson, which is always the best place to start. W*hy should I teach this?* The authors answer by explaining how this clinic will help the writer grow, as well as how it will help the writer meet the standards. They link each clinic to the corresponding Common Core anchor standards and offer suggestions for what to do prior to the lesson to prepare kids for the experience. The book provides step-by-step guidance with teaching notes for each slide; the images on the slides themselves guide the class through the clinic, giving kids time to talk, time to work together, time to write, and time to share. The slides are visually compelling, the directions clear, the models supportive. One of my favorite clinics is titled "The Found Poem: Finding the Unusual in the Usual." Michael looks in a hardware store, writes down what he sees, and shows kids how he turns that list into a poem. What a great way for kids to start looking more closely at their world and thinking of it in a slightly different way.

The truth is that as I write this foreword, I am turning slightly green with envy. I really wish I had written this resource. Having read it, it is tough not to be jealous. But the truth is I couldn't have written it; only poets could write this— and specifically only Sara and Michael. I can't wait to use this resource to teach kids how to write clearly, concisely, and cleverly and to help them see poetry in a new and different light. I encourage you to jump right into *High-Impact Writing Clinics.* Your kids will thrive. They can be themselves. And they will become far better writers who will not only meet, but exceed, the standards. I love this resource, and so will you. Happy reading and viewing!

—*Stephanie Harvey*

Introduction

For poems are not, as people think, simply emotions (one has emotions early enough)—they are experiences.

—Rainer Maria Rilke

Flying

Writing for me is like flying,
without the white knuckles,
without the bad food
and the too-tight seat buckles.
I skim across clouds
losing track of the hours,
touch goose-feather down
all unfazed by the showers.

Writing for me is both wide-winged
and wingless,
like bees and like wasps
with a sting and yet stingless.
My bones have no pith,
they are hollow and light.
Words flood through the corridors,
day into night.

This is for me, the best of all flight,
When I sit in my chair—just sit there
and write.

—Jane Yolen

High-Impact Writing Clinics will get kids writing.

We share your goals for student writers: to empower them with first-rate communication skills that will benefit them in school and, later, in college and career. Over the past 20 years, we have taught writing workshops in schools in almost every one of the United States and 30 other countries to kids in urban and rural communities, of diverse ethnic and economic backgrounds, and to kids who are speaking English as an additional language. We teach kids who look straight at us and say, "I can't write," while sitting elbow to elbow with kids who say, "I love to write." We believe *all* of these student writers—and their busy teachers—will benefit from these writing clinics.

As we work in classrooms almost every week of the school year, we are intimately familiar with the pressures put on both English and content area teachers to increase students' literacy skills while simultaneously developing their understanding of complex subject matter. With the adoption of the Common Core State Standards (CCSS), this pressure has increased even more. We built the lessons in this book and on the accompanying DVD to help ease that pressure. These clinics enable students to demonstrate their knowledge of content through detailed and focused writing. From predicting, to synthesizing, to summarizing, these clinics show students *how* to showcase this understanding clearly and concisely. Each clinic teaches students to recognize components of effective writing and then provides them with guided practice employing those same elements in fast and focused writing assignments. As students learn to recognize—and appreciate—elements of craft, they become habitually close readers in the process. The writing students produce will also enable you to get a quick snapshot of what they know and are able to do, thus providing you with an ongoing tool for formative assessment.

Being poets, we naturally gravitated toward this form when developing these writing clinics in classrooms. But being poets, we also know how scary the word *poetry* can be for a teacher who hasn't had a whole lot of experience with the genre, especially if you are teaching social studies, history, math, or science. If you count yourself among this reticent group, rest assured these writing clinics are designed to make it easier for you to incorporate writing into your lesson plans across content areas. They also happen to be both practical and fun.

If you are a true poetry fan (we know there are a bunch of you out there), these clinics will help you bring this precise and concise writing format into your classroom in a manner that will satisfy even the most standards-frazzled administrator.

HOW DO THE PROJECTABLE LESSONS AND BOOK WORK?

These 20 clinics—projectable lessons provided for you on DVD—will help you address the CCSS for Literacy in English Language Arts, History/ Social Studies, Science, and Technical Subjects by engaging students in writing designed to improve essential skills, such as how to persuade or argue effectively in writing. Each lesson focuses on one or two writing skills and asks students to write nonfiction poetry about language arts or content area learning, offering you opportunities to teach and reteach essential communication and literacy skills. The lessons are designed for use in intermediate and middle grade-level classrooms (Grades 4–8); however, many of the lessons are readily adaptable for younger or older students with a little tweaking by a classroom teacher.

You will find the ready-to-go lessons on projectable slides on the DVD in the back of this book. The slide presentations are for use *during the lesson*. They attach images to the concepts for your students, which is especially helpful for visual learners.

In the book, you will find a step-by-step guide for the lesson you are teaching. These presenter notes also include suggestions that we have gleaned from teaching these lessons in the classroom.

Adjacent to each step in the book is a thumbnail of the corresponding slide, so it is easy to see where you are. The material in this book also provides the following:

- **Why Teach This?** a rationale for each lesson
- **CCSS and Corresponding Anchor Standards**: a list of the many standards the lesson helps students meet
- **Prior to the Lesson**: a short list of things to consider or do before you begin teaching the lesson

The book and slides work together and are ready to use after a quick review.

In addition to the projectable lessons, the DVD contains a searchable spreadsheet with hyperlinks to the individual lessons. You can use this feature to search the lessons based on the following:

- Purpose
- Common Core State Standards the lesson addresses
- Content area(s) the lesson applies to

THE PROJECTABLE LESSONS

In each projectable lesson, you will find the following:

What Are We Going to Learn Today?

- Questions for the class to consider during the lesson.

Text Talk

- A mentor text to share with the class, including an audio recording of a poet reading the text. (You may wish to invite your students to compare the spoken word to the written word.)
- Possible discussion points and questions.

Work Together

- In this section you work together as a class. Step-by-step instructions guide you and students through the process of composing a similar poem collaboratively.

Time to Write

- In pairs or small groups, students compose their own similar poem.
- Step-by-step instructions help you lead your class through this writing process.

Share

- Student volunteers share their work. We provide a variety of ways to make this speaking and listening portion of the lesson fun.

Take Away

- A quick review for students of skills they practiced during the clinic.

Bonus Poems

- Two or more poems that can be used to extend the lesson. We offer simpler and more complex poems, so you can differentiate according to the needs of your students. These can also be used to serve as models for subsequent writing and/or publication. Often these poems are more sophisticated examples of the skill being practiced in the clinic, showing students the technique being used by real writers in real texts.

HOW DO THESE LESSONS FIT IN CONTENT AREA CLASSROOMS?

Throughout the lessons we share writing samples from content area classrooms that implemented these lessons. This does not mean that any particular lesson is intended to be confined to any one content area. Just because the lesson on couplets uses a sample poem that references the brain and nervous system doesn't mean that the teacher may not wish to use couplets to describe fractions (math), characterizations (fiction), or an event in history (social studies).

HOW DO THESE WRITING CLINICS FIT WITH OTHER WRITING PROGRAMS?

These clinics do not constitute a complete writing syllabus. Although the lessons and their curriculum goals are robust enough to stand on their own, we believe they can be most useful as a plug-in to whatever program you are currently using, whether it is prepackaged or of your own design. We're not asking you to toss out everything you've been doing; instead, we are offering classroom-tested methods and lessons for teaching the components that are integral in all good writing programs. If you equate your current writing program to a blueprint for building a new garden shed, count our 20 writing clinics among the lumber and hardware.

Most important, we believe your students will find these writing clinics fun and engaging, and that you will find them easy to use, as we have found when we've taught them in schools.

HOW DO THE LESSONS HELP STUDENTS MEET THE CCSS?

Throughout the standards we see an emphasis on exposing students to a variety of language experiences, poetry included. Rather than relegating poetry to holidays, love, and angst—a writing activity to be done before or after the real work of school—poetry takes its proper place alongside other genres of writing.

We have identified CCSS standards specific to every writing clinic (see the spreadsheet on the DVD and the lists in each lesson in this book). Below, we have identified some key skills and standards from the CCSS that are addressed in our lessons.

Details, Details, Details

From RL.1 to L.6., at all grade levels one word pops up over and over: *details*. Details to support arguments, to demonstrate evidence, to describe, to make points of comparison, and to make points that help readers identify the themes and reasoning contained in increasingly complex texts. Poetry is language rendered down to the most essential details, precise language stated in the most concise way. Poetry does not let you get away with saying, "The sunset was beautiful." It requires *detailed* descriptors. Repeated practice using precise detail is perhaps the most important benefit of these writing clinics.

Argument and Persuasion

W.1, for all grade levels, states that students will *develop and write arguments to support claims in analysis of substantive topics or texts*. This skill is not only essential in terms of meeting the CCSS but is also essential in life. How often do you hear students argue that something is *awesome* or *awkward* in the misguided belief that they have stated a valid argument? We thought this skill so important that we put it in the very first writing clinic (Objective Versus Subjective). The precise nature of poetry demands a clear understanding of the difference between facts and opinions. Practicing this skill in a small poem will help build students' persuasive prowess. From predicting, to synthesizing, to summarizing, these clinics show students how to showcase their understanding through clear and concise composition.

Close Reading

Close—or careful—reading is critical in the development of thoughtful students and citizens. Skimming may be fine for light fiction, but not when it comes to the fine print on a mortgage or instructions about the safe handling of a chainsaw. Mark Twain once said, "Be careful about reading health books. You may die of a misprint." Nobody wants that! But we don't want any students to die of in-depth analysis either. That's why a short poem is a perfect place to practice careful reading.

As schools and teachers scramble to find ways to meet the new CCSS, guidelines and suggestions have been published on the Internet. As educator Dea Conrad-Curry, PhD, suggests on her blog (http://dconrad3.wordpress.com/2012/07/), close reading calls on the students' ability to answer the following questions when reading a text:

1. What does the speaker explicitly state as the purpose for this occasion?
2. What comparison or analogy is most prominently developed throughout this text?
3. Why is this analogy important to the overall meaning of this text?
4. In light of the analogy developed, what is the actual and yet implicit purpose of this text?

"The purpose of close reading should not be a function in itself," she states, "but in developing appreciation for the universal and timeless value innate to complex texts and worthy of the classroom investment." When we read her essay (definitely worth reading in its entirety), we wrote to ask her if she believed the reading of poetry to be a valid place to practice careful reading. She replied:

> Poetry is the perfect vehicle for teaching close reading. The preciseness of diction, the tightness of form, the eloquence of thought—resulting in unique qualia—are all indeed aspects for consideration in close reading. . . . [A]s I work with teachers on understanding the importance of attending to the details of pronouns, antecedents, and transitions, I find many are as confused as students in making connections between and among such words. Poets use these very tools of grammar to arrive at the necessary precision.

In addition to the mentor texts provided in each lesson, the bonus poems at the end of each lesson can be used to practice close reading.

Poems Value Evidence

Anchor Standard 1 calls for students to cite/use specific textual evidence as they read and write. The lessons in this book and on the DVD teach students how to create poetry by selecting relevant details. They also show students how their points may be best supported by *facts* in their writing and speaking. After building their own poems out of evidential details, students become better able to cite how other authors make their reasoning (evidence) clear to a reader or listener. Further, each lesson's Share segment allows students to hear what some of their peers have written. A post-performance discussion can lead to students actively evaluating others' use of evidence.

Speaking and Listening

SL.1 states that students should *engage effectively in a range of collaborative discussion one-on-one, in groups, and teacher led with diverse partners on grade[-level appropriate] topics and texts, building on others' ideas and expressing their own clearly.* Each of our writing clinics engage students in collaborative discussion throughout—listening to their classmates and actively responding—in most cases before they ever put pen to paper or hands to keyboard, whichever the case may be.

Also, because every lesson is completed with a Share session, students are able to practice their speaking and active listening skills in frequent brief exchanges. This frequency is purposeful as it builds confidence in speakers. One speech to be delivered at the end of the school year can be terribly intimidating; 20 short poetry presentations provide an opportunity for students to practice skills such as voice projection, inflection, and stance on a continual basis, which is much less threatening.

The Importance of Writing Routinely

As teaching poets, we often compare writing to golf when we talk to students. The more practice strokes you make, the better your game. No golfers make par on their first round. Athletes, just like writers, benefit from repeated instruction and coaching. Even pros seek out clinics to improve technique, learning how to make the ball go where they want it to go in as few strokes as possible. Writing, like golf, is about accuracy, efficiency, and a little finesse. But by personally practicing the game, one is better equipped to appreciate a good performance and critique a poor one. The same is just as true in writing. These writing clinics will keep students in the game, writing their way to a better understanding of literary techniques and content area understanding (Anchor Standard 10). In these lessons, we routinely ask students to employ the very same conventions that they are asked to identify in their reading of text. The result? Students become more careful, critical readers, like the writers they have become.

The most important thing about these clinics is that they will help kids continue to improve their literacy skills and content area understanding through regular, focused writing workshops.

WHY POETRY?

Below, we list many further benefits of using these lessons—and poetry in general—to teach literacy skills.

Writing Poetry Demonstrates Independence

- Poems are short text, a snapshot of a topic. Snapshot reading, writing, and performance enable students to build independence using manageable text.

- Poetry is not only an art form or an artifact of learning; it is a tool for acquiring knowledge and understanding.

- As students read, write, and perform poetry, they take an active role in their own learning.

- Performing poetry helps students with reading fluency as it requires repeated reading.

- Reading and writing poetry naturally builds academic vocabulary as students read, reread, and discuss a poem's meaning.

Writing Poetry About Nonfiction Content Strengthens Knowledge and Understanding

- Poems are concise, informational text that students may use to build and convey content knowledge.

- Writing and performing poetry about content area learning helps students predict, synthesize, and retell what they are learning.

- Student poetry is a quick assessment of the writer's level of discipline-specific expertise.

- Poetry is an effective and efficient way for students to share their knowledge and teach others through writing and speaking.

Performing Poetry Requires Students to Respond to the Varying Demands of Audience, Task, Purpose, and Discipline

- Performing poetry helps students learn how to better communicate face to face with an audience.

- Performing poetry is an ideal way for students to see how communication and word connotation are affected by tone and inflection.

- Writing with performance in mind affords students the opportunity to craft their writing to fit both the content of the poem and the audience.

- Classroom performance builds both speaking and listening skills as students continually practice their oral presentation and active listening abilities.

- The lessons themselves can be seen as models of how to use visual displays in presentations and can themselves be discussion starters.

Writing Poetry Increases Comprehension and Engagement

- Introducing poetry performance into the classroom engages students as readers, writers, and listeners.

- Discussion of a poem helps students comprehend more precisely what the author is saying by reading closely and carefully, and allows them to do this work with a relatively short text.

- Collaboration in the writing and performing of poetry helps students comprehend as they discuss their short texts together and revise individual words, seeking to clarify meaning before they say it aloud.

Poetry Leads Students to Understand Other Perspectives and Cultures

- Through performing poetry (see the Bonus Poems section of each lesson), students give voice to great classical and contemporary works of literature as they vicariously inhabit worlds and have experiences much different than their own.

- By composing poetry for multiple voices, students create written pieces that show diverse perspectives.

- When students perform historical poetry, they are bringing to life a variety of first person narratives; this can deepen their understanding of diverse experiences and perspectives.

- Working together to compose and perform poetry will help students communicate and work with others of varied backgrounds, as students learn to appreciate perspective and diversity.

WHAT ABOUT ASSESSMENT?

The true test of the effectiveness of these writing clinics will be in the students' writing as they put these individual skills into practice in *all* of their writing. The lessons should not end when the clinic is over; they should serve as touchstones as you confer with students (and they confer with each other) about other pieces of writing they are composing. This will enable you to say, for example, "Remember that writing clinic we had on visual language? I would like to see more of that visual language when I read your essay on the Civil War."

It is possible that the writing produced in these clinics might be revised and developed into more complex pieces of writing also. As the poems students compose are added to their portfolios, they will become drafts that the students might select to polish, augment, and refine into an essay or a story.

Sara: Is that enough? Can we just leave it there?

Michael: Nope.

Sara: But we don't expect each of these clinics to produce writing that will be repeatedly revised, conferred upon, and published. A few maybe, but mostly these are like scales: You do them and then apply the skills to more complex text.

Michael: True. But we still need a way to help teachers evaluate student success on these tasks.

Sara: Rubrics might take some of the hesitancy out of poetry assessment that teachers may have.

Michael: Right. The key to assessment is setting goals in advance of the lesson and then measuring student progress against those goals. Rubrics can help set these goals.

A sample rubric for assessment would look like the one on the facing page. We include one of these in each lesson in this book. This one is for Clinic 5: Feelings Made Visual; in it, students write a poem using mentor text, incorporating visual language as they describe feelings, use gerunds correctly, and conclude their poem with a couplet, thereby demonstrating their understanding of the word *couplet*.

We have anticipated what some criteria for the assessment might be, while expecting that you will make additions and changes to the rubrics based on your own classroom goals. For instance, if students will be using a particular clinic to write about their current unit of study, say the American Bison (see Clinic 7), you will want to assess their ability not only to follow a writing pattern using strong details, but also to demonstrate an understanding of the plight of the bison over the past couple of centuries. Poetry is not "just writing what you feel." It is also writing what is true, and as such can be both a vehicle for learning and a quick assessment tool.

As professional writers, we are learning every day. In designing these clinics, we did our best to set the tone that we are joining you and your class as writers. It is a long path for anyone to find their voice through writing. Our hope is that if we share our writing strategies with students, these techniques will help them find and refine their own voices.

From activating and assessing prior knowledge to summarizing learning, these writing clinics are designed to get kids thinking about their writing craft as well as their content area learning, thereby deepening and increasing their understanding of concepts in English language arts and across the curriculum.

Skill	3	2	1
Careful Reading	Demonstrates, through classroom discussion and writing, an understanding of the impact of word choice on meaning and tone.	Partially demonstrates, through classroom discussion and writing, an understanding of the impact of word choice on meaning and tone. May include a single detail in the final piece that may not seem relevant to the piece.	Does not demonstrate, through classroom discussion and writing, an understanding of the impact of word choice on meaning and tone.
Structure and Organization	Demonstrates the ability to recognize and re-create a writing structure, such as a strong conclusion.	Partially demonstrates the ability to recognize and re-create a writing structure, such as a strong conclusion. May make a single comparison that may not seem logical or may not be backed by objective observations.	Does not demonstrate the ability to recognize and re-create a writing structure, such as a strong conclusion.
Grammar Conventions	Demonstrates an understanding of how to use nouns and gerund verbs in the analysis and writing of poetry.	Partially demonstrates an understanding of how to use nouns and gerund verbs in the analysis and writing of poetry. May make a minor grammatical error.	Does not demonstrate an understanding of how to use nouns and gerund verbs in the analysis and writing of poetry.
Connotative Word Meaning	Demonstrates an understanding of connotative word meanings when using visual language to describe a feeling.	Occasionally demonstrates an understanding of the connotative word meanings when using visual language to describe a feeling. May make a comparison that does not seem logical or is not backed by objective evidence.	Does not demonstrate an understanding of connotative word meanings when using visual language to describe a feeling.
Speaking Skills	Consistently demonstrates effective presentation skills using good voice projection, inflection, pacing, eye contact, and stance.	Partially demonstrates effective presentation skills using good voice projection, inflection, pacing, eye contact, and stance.	Does not demonstrate effective presentation skills using good voice projection, inflection, pacing, eye contact, and stance.
Listening Skills	Actively participates in discussions about other students' work and is tuned in to student presentations.	Occasionally participates in discussions about other students' work and is tuned in to student presentations.	Does not participate in discussions about other students' work and is not tuned in to student presentations.

We share your goals for student writers: to empower them with first-rate communication skills that will benefit them in school and in the world. In these lessons we are building skills that reach well beyond the English language arts classroom, as students use poetry not simply as a forum for writing about their feelings, but also as a means to write about content from a wide range of subject areas.

Echoing Jane Yolen's poem, we want our students' writing to take off and fly.

We look forward to joining you in your classroom. Let's get writing!

We would like to dedicate the book to Suzi Creamcheese, Lilith Soufflé, and Uncle Hector for their patience in walks postponed during the writing of this book. But not to Spike. Definitely not to Spike.

Writing Clinics

1

Objective Versus Subjective

Making Sense of Opinions

WHY TEACH THIS?

Good writers use objective evidence to support opinions. In this clinic students will strengthen their abilities to recognize unsubstantiated opinions and correct them in their own writing. This important life skill is essential as students create persuasive arguments and detailed content area reports.

Opinion words (aka subjective terms) are not effective in the writing of fiction, literary nonfiction, poetry, and historical or scientific texts. Too often students will write something such as "The sunset was gorgeous" or "The civil war was hard" without including objective observations as to why this is so. This is why we also refer to subjective terms as *first draft words*.

Kids want to be heard. They want others to listen to their opinions and ideas. In order for them to be heard and understood, they need to provide detailed, objective reasoning for their observations. This clinic will help students make their points, backed with irrefutable evidence.

Additionally, this poetry writing exercise will help strengthen students' critical reading skills, enhancing their ability to recognize subjective and objective observations in text written by others.

Michael: We will be referring back to this concept over and over again throughout these clinics.

Sara: Understanding the difference between fact and opinion is basic to all kinds of writing: scientific, fiction, nonfiction, and—most certainly—poetry.

CCSS AND CORRESPONDING ANCHOR STANDARDS

- **Demonstrate** understanding of word relationships, and nuances in word meanings.

  [4.L.5] [5.L.5] [6.L.5] [7.L.5] [8.L.5]

- **Determine** central ideas or themes of a text and analyze their development; summarize the key supporting details and ideas.

  [4.RIT.2] [5.RIT.2] [6.RIT.2] [7.RIT.2] [8.RIT.2]

- **Delineate** and evaluate the argument and specific claims in a text, including the validity of the reasoning as well as the relevance and the sufficiency of the evidence.

  [4.RIT.8] [5.RIT.8] [6.RIT.8] [7.RIT.8] [8.RIT.8]

- **Interpret** words and phrases as they are used in a text, including determining technical, connotative, and figurative meanings, and analyze how specific word choices shape meaning or tone.

  [4.RL.4] [5.RL.4] [6.RL.4] [7.RL.4] [8.RL.4]

- **Assess** how point of view or purpose shapes the content and style of text.

  [4.RL.6] [5.RL.6] [6.RL.6] [7.RL.6] [8.RL.6]

- **Read** and comprehend complex literary and informational texts independently and proficiently.

  [4.RL.10] [5.RL.10] [6.RL.10] [7.RL.10] [8.RL.10]

- **Integrate** and evaluate information presented in diverse media and formats, including visually, quantitatively, and orally.

  [4.SL.2] [5.SL.2] [6.SL.2] [7.SL.2] [8.SL.2]

- **Write** narrative to develop real or imagined experiences or events using effective technique, well-chosen details, and well-structured sequences.

  [4.W.3] [5.W.3] [6.W.3] [7.W.3] [8.W.3]

- **Produce** clear and coherent writing in which the development, organization, and style are appropriate to task, purpose, and audience.

  [4.W.4] [5.W.4] [6.W.4] [7.W.4] [8.W.4]

PRIOR TO THE LESSON

- Read through the entire lesson and review the slideshow to familiarize yourself with the clinic.

- You may find that one of the bonus poems at the end of this clinic is better suited to your class as an example text than the one embedded in the clinic. This is your choice.

- Set up a separate surface (chart paper or white board) on which to compose a poem that will be written collectively by you and your students.

THE LESSON

Slide 1

- Introduce the teaching poets by name (Sara and Michael), as they will appear throughout this writing clinic.

Slides 2–3

- Read aloud or have a student read through the clinic goals.
- Review the purpose of the lesson and then ask students to turn and talk about why they think this may be important.
- Ask: Why is it important to support our opinions with facts? Why is this important in school and in life?
- Ask: What is the difference between a fact and an opinion?
- Ask to hear a couple student responses aloud.
- This chat to start the lesson will allow you to gauge prior knowledge.

Slide 4

- Everyone has opinions; they begin at birth. Children cry when they don't get the food or attention they want when they want it.
- Prove your point by throwing out some controversial idea, such as school uniforms, cell phones in class, or the name of a teen idol, and watch the classroom explode with opinions.
- Respond that while you hear their opinions, students must also provide concrete details to substantiate these opinions in order to form an effective argument.

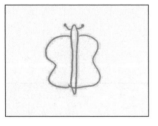

Slide 5

- Ask kids what they think.
- Ask: What is this? (Hopefully at least one student will recognize this crude drawing as a butterfly.)
- Ask: Is this a real butterfly? The answer is no. It is an image of a butterfly.

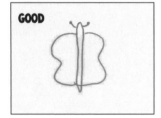

Slide 6

- Say something like: Some people would look at this image of a butterfly and say that it is good. They have seen butterflies, they don't bite, and they are pretty.
- Explain that their opinion would be that this image of a butterfly is GOOD.

Slide 7

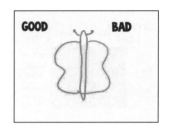

- Say something like: Other people would look at the image of the butterfly and say, "Are you kidding me? This is the worst drawing of a butterfly I have ever seen in my life!"
- Explain that their opinion would be that this image is BAD.

Slide 8

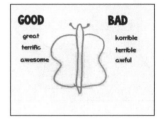

- Say something like: If I see a word like *good* in a piece of student writing, I always ask the writer, "Can you be more specific?" Likewise with the word *bad*. It doesn't help to just substitute other opinion words such as *awful* or *terrible*.
- You have probably told your students this repeatedly. It is okay to be an I-told-you-so here. You may even have recent examples to cite.
- Ask the students to brainstorm four or five more synonyms for the words *good* and *bad*. Words might include *fabulous, dreadful, wonderful, appalling, outstanding,* and *atrocious*.

Slide 9

- Explain that words such as these are known as "subjective terms."
- Discuss the difference between the words *subjective* (opinions) and *objective* (evidence).
  - A *subjective* term is an opinion.
  - An *objective* term is a verifiable fact.
- Ask: Can you think of a reason why we cannot simply rely on opinions in our writing? Is this only true in poetry? Is it also true in other types of writing? Discuss.

Slide 10

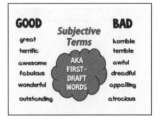

- Ask: Why do you think that the poets call subjective terms *first draft words*? (Because often on first drafts, we are working quickly, knowing we will have the opportunity to clarify and revise later.)

Slide 11

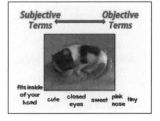

- Ask students which of these descriptors for the puppy are subjective (opinions) and which are objective (facts).
- Ask the students to brainstorm other subjective and objective descriptors for the puppy.

Slide 12

- Note that it is fair to use opinions in our writing IF we back up those opinions with objective evidence, like this:
  - Her pink nose was so cute.
  - The way she closed her eyes was sweet.
  - She was so tiny, she fit in my hand.

Slide 13

- Read these additional thoughts from Sara and Michael.
- Explain that often student writers will say something like "The sunset was terrific" in a first draft.
- Tell students that as they work with a partner, with a writing coach, or on their own, they can revise their writing to support an opinion with substantive details.

Slide 14

- Using our senses will help us to be more objective and therefore more descriptive in our writing.
- Point out to the students that not only will this help them to write better poetry, but it will also help them in their persuasive and content area writing.
- Example: Saying that a marble rolls *fast* on an incline is not a precise, scientific observation. It is just an opinion. What objective information would you need to substantiate the word *fast*?

Text Talk

Slide 15

- Tell students they will be using their senses to analyze the piece in front of them.
- Ask: Which is it? Do these sensory details describe something that is good or bad?
- Discuss how a phrase such as *spoiled milk* might be used as evidence to support the opinion that a situation is bad.
- Inform students that this piece is Version 1 and that they will be revisiting it to revise later.

Work Together

Slide 16

- Choose which term to write about as a group: GOOD or BAD.
- Let the students vote.
- Compose a poem together as a class, using a separate surface for writing space. Ask students to describe their chosen word using sensory details (as in Slide 15).

- Make sure that the sensory details do NOT include more opinion words, as they do in this example: "Bad smells horrible."

- Ask: What smells bad and why? Spoiled fish? Moldy socks?

- Alert the students to watch out for clichés.

- Reminder: A cliché is a widely known expression that, once begun, can be completed by someone else: e.g., a deer in the _____; nails on a _____.

- Urge students to think beyond clichés by saying: What sounds as bad as nails on a chalkboard? Clichés can be stepping stones to precise and original language.

Time to Write

Slide 17

- Time to write individually.

- Have students get out their writer's notebooks, laptops, or pieces of paper.

- Ask each student to choose an opinion word (aka a subjective term) so they can come up with their own sensory details that describe that word. (See Slide 18 for ideas.)

Slide 18

- Have students choose a subjective term to write about.

- See the list of suggested opinion words.

- Students may choose words other than these, but you will want to check in and make sure that the words are truly opinion words, and not definitive nouns or verbs (e.g., *chair, run*).

- Check to make sure that no one chooses an inappropriate or unkind word (e.g., *retarded, spastic*).

- Consider having students choose from a list of different subjective terms— ones that you have preselected.

- Prompt students to use more challenging opinion words (e.g., *exceptional, atrocious*), as needed.

- Note that these words may masquerade as more sophisticated writing. Opinions are opinions, whether they have one syllable or three.

Slide 19

- Use these sensory terms to prompt the students as they write.

- Walk them through these prompts one at a time.

- Check in and ask two or three students to read their responses aloud after each prompt. This will help students who are struggling.

- Encourage students to ask each other for ideas if they become stuck.

- Understand that this is a lively writing process and that students will benefit from being able to bounce ideas around.

- Note: We always wind up having to make some restrictions about potty talk. Basically, we tell the kids that poop talk is lazy language. Describing something bad as "It tastes like poop" is overused and therefore is not as effective as saying something tastes like day-old stinky cat food.

Slide 20

- Have the students share their drafts with a partner.
- Consider having students turn to another table or find a new partner with whom to share.
- If they have been sharing with the same students throughout the writing process, instruct students to listen in order to ensure that their partner has used objective sensory data.

Time to Revise

Slide 21

- Revisit BAD Version 1.
- Bring students' attention back to our Version 1 Text Talk poem about the subjective word, *bad*.
- Tell students that it's time to revise.

Slide 22

- Revisit BAD Version 2.
- Strike out the sensory words by drawing lines through them.
- Don't erase or black out, as students may decide later that they want one or two of the words back.
- Read the remaining words.
- Explain to students that this is starting to sound like a poem, but that they are not there yet. Tell students that this is what we call a poem skeleton.
- Ask: What is a skeleton? What does it do? What is it missing? (It is a framework. It is missing connective tissue.)
- Explain: Let's add some transition words and maybe rearrange the lines to see what kind of magic we can create from this skeleton.

Slide 23

- This is BAD busted up.
- Ask: What happens if we bust up the lines?
- Ask students whether they can see some ideas for putting them back together, and invite them to discuss various options.
- The next slide shows what Sara and Michael did with the lines; but before you go to that, see what ideas your students might have.

Slide 24

- Read through BAD Version 3.

- Note that the added words are in red. Discuss how those transition words stitch the poem together.

- Explain to students that if they have written strong, objective details, they will have good building blocks for writing their poems.

- Note how in this example, we kept the sensory phrase *feels like*. Writers may decide to keep a different phrase or none. There are no right or wrong choices, but students will want to be logical.

Share

Slide 25

- Have the students share their drafts with a partner.

- Consider having partners turn to another table or find a new partner with whom to share if they have been sharing with the same students throughout the writing process.

- Instruct students to listen in order to ensure that their partner has used objective sensory data.

- Have students share their writing with the class.

- Reinforce good examples as you hear them. Every student will come up with at least a few good lines, and some will be off-the-charts great!

- Discuss as you move along how certain lines would be effective if dropped into a science report, a story, or an expository essay.

Slide 26

- Indicate that this writing clinic will be a touchstone for students as they work on revisions of future pieces of writing.

- Tell students that they should ask themselves or others in their writing groups to support their opinions with objective details. Remind them that these details may include sensory references.

- Explain: It is unlikely that you will ever use all of your senses for one subjective term, as we did here.

- Explain: In this exercise we were stretching to open our minds to possibilities.

Slide 27

- Reinforce that we are not just talking about supporting our opinions when it comes to poetry, but that this is something that's important in all types of writing.

- Note that in science class, this is the difference between evidence and interpretation.

Bonus Poems and Lesson Extensions

Slide 28

- These bonus poems have been selected to give you the opportunity to differentiate the needs of your classroom and to extend and reinforce the lesson.

Slide 29: "Gruesome" by Michael Salinger

- Read the poem aloud, have a student read it, and/or play the audio.
- Ask: What objective details does Salinger use to describe the word *gruesome*?
- Have students turn and talk about which details are effective and why.
- Note: Michael took this picture in Sedlec, Czech Republic, at an ossuary. It is a church decorated with skeletal remains from the plague. More information about this gruesome place is available online.

Slide 30: "On a Winter's Night" by Susan Campbell Bartoletti

- Read the poem aloud, have a student read it, and/or play the audio.
- Ask: Does the author use primarily subjective or objective language in this poem? (Objective.)
- Note: The poet doesn't assign any particular feeling or opinions to her observation.
- Ask: Thinking subjectively, to what feeling might the light from the lamppost refer? (The light from the lamppost might stand for comfort, hope, isolation.) Discuss possible answers with your students. Note that there are no right or wrong answers.
- Note: Susan Campbell Bartoletti is an award-winning author of nonfiction books. She also writes poetry from her backyard snuggery in Scranton, Pennsylvania. For more information about Susan and her dynamic career, please visit her website at www.scbartoletti.com.

Slide 31: "One Hot Hound" by Larry Dane Brimner

- Read the poem aloud, have a student read it, and/or play the audio.
- Note: This poem is a Haiku. (Japanese form: five syllables, seven syllables, five syllables.)
- Ask: What is happening in this poem? (A dog meets a sprinkler at the hottest time of the day.)
- Ask: What does the poet mean by the word *conversing*? (The dog and the sprinkler are mixing it up.)
- Note: Haiku poems are very succinct, clarifying images through objective facts.

- Note: Larry Dane Brimner is a dog lover who has written a lot of books—big books, little books, and in-between books. Always fun and full of facts, he is the recipient of numerous awards for his writing of nonfiction. You can find out more about Larry, his books, school visits, and teacher workshops at www.brimner.com.

Slide 32: "My Official List" by Sara Holbrook

- Explain that this is a poem intended for two voices.
- Read it with another student, have two students read it, and/or play the accompanying audio.
- Ask students if "My Official List" comprises subjective or objective details.
- Suggest to students that perhaps they would like to make their own "official list" poems composed of objective details.

Slide 33–36: "The Blind Men and the Elephant" by John Godfrey Saxe

- Introduce the poet and the concept of writing a poem version of a story.
- Share this background information:
  - The poem is based on an Indian folk tale. Go to www.jainworld.com/literature/story25.htm to compare the original tale to the poem.
  - It was written by John Godfrey Saxe (1816–1867), an American from Vermont.
  - It is perhaps the quintessential tale of opinions superseding facts.
- Read the poem aloud, have students split up the verses (nine in all) and read it, and/or play the audio.
- Click on the link to hear a rendition of the poem or go to http://www.youtube.com/watch?v=iBqgr5xZLz0.
- After reading through the entire poem (and/or listening to the audio or musical version), note that the last verse is the moral of the story.
- Ask students to turn and talk, discussing what they believe the moral of the story to be.
- Ask: Could you rewrite your own moral to the story?

ASSESSMENT

Here we provide a rubric you may choose to use. We provide this as a guide knowing that you may have other goals for your class. Don't feel compelled to assess every skill mentioned in this chart. We have had more success when we zero in on a skill or two with a lesson, but we want to afford you multiple options with these clinics.

Skill	3	2	1
Fact Versus Opinion	Demonstrates understanding of the difference between fact and opinion.	Partially demonstrates understanding of the difference between fact and opinion. May identify a subjective term as an objective term but is correct the majority of the time.	Does not distinguish between fact and opinion.
Supporting Factual Details	Effectively supports opinions with concrete reasoning.	Partially develops a narrative story using the prescribed pattern. Some supporting details are subjective while the majority of them are objective.	Does not develop a narrative story using the prescribed pattern.
Revision: The Abbreviation	Effectively recognizes and eliminates the sensory terms in the first revision.	Partially recognizes and eliminates the sensory terms in the first revision.	Does not recognize or eliminate the sensory terms in the first revision.
Revision: Adding Transition Words and Phrases	Demonstrates an understanding of transition words and phrases and uses them to make the poem coherent.	Partially demonstrates an understanding of transition words and phrases and begins to use them to make the poem coherent. Some transitions may not be smooth or may be missing.	Does not demonstrate an understanding of transition words and phrases and is unable to use them to make the poem coherent.
Author's Craft	Demonstrates through classroom discussion and writing an understanding of how an author uses reason and evidence to support particular points.	Partially demonstrates through classroom discussion and writing an understanding of how an author uses reason and evidence to support particular points.	Does not demonstrate through classroom discussion and writing an understanding of how an author uses reason and evidence to support particular points.
Speaking Skills	Consistently demonstrates effective presentation skills using good voice projection, inflection, pacing, eye contact, and stance.	Partially demonstrates effective presentation skills using good voice projection, inflection, pacing, eye contact, and stance.	Does not demonstrate effective presentation skills using good voice projection, inflection, pacing, eye contact, and stance.
Listening Skills	Actively participates in discussions of other students' work and is tuned in to student presentations.	Occasionally participates in discussions of other students' work and is somewhat tuned in to student presentations.	Does not participate in discussions of other students' work and is not tuned in to student presentations.

2

The List Poem

WHY TEACH THIS?

Lists are how we remember what needs remembering. Whether we're headed to the grocery store and don't want to forget the cilantro or we're gearing up for a vacation trip, lists are a familiar format for students. Lists also provide us with the opportunity to check things off as we complete tasks and give us the chance to weigh and prioritize the importance of ideas, objects, or events.

There are three key benefits of teaching list poems to students:

1. It is instructive to students to see the usefulness of listing details in advance of any type of writing.

2. Writing a list poem about current studies deepens students' understanding of the elements of any subject matter.

3. Lists help students remember.

So, when is a list of words a poem? When we call it a poem, that's when! Some list poems rhyme, some don't. Some have refrains, some don't. Some have rhythm . . . well, you get the picture. You really can't go wrong with a list poem as long as it is composed of concrete details.

Sara: Lists lead to lively writing—it's all in the details.

Michael: I often start my pieces with a list; this allows me to sift through the details. I have to gather and pick the very best ones.

CCSS AND CORRESPONDING ANCHOR STANDARDS

- **Demonstrate** understanding of figurative language, word relationships, and nuances in word meanings.

  [4.L.5] [5.L.5] [6.L.5] [7.L.5] [8.L.5]

- **Interpret** words and phrases as they are used in a text, including determining technical, connotative, and figurative meanings, and analyze how specific word choices shape meaning or tone.

  [4.RIT.4] [5.RIT.4] [6.RIT.4] [7.RIT.4] [8.RIT.4]

- **Read** and comprehend complex literary and informational texts independently and proficiently.

  [4.RL.10] [5.RL.10] [6.RL.10] [7.RL.10] [8.RL.10]

- **Integrate** and evaluate information presented in diverse media and formats, including visually, quantitatively, and orally.

  [4.SL.2] [5.SL.2] [6.SL.2] [7.SL.2] [8.SL.2]

- **Write** informative/explanatory texts to examine and convey complex ideas and information clearly and accurately through the effective selection, organization, and analysis of content.

  [4.W.2] [5.W.2] [6.W.2] [7.W.2] [8.W.2]

- **Produce** clear and coherent writing in which the development, organization, and style are appropriate to task, purpose, and audience.

  [4.W.4] [5.W.4] [6.W.4] [7.W.4] [8.W.4]

- **Gather** relevant information from multiple print and digital sources, assess the credibility and accuracy of each source, and integrate the information while avoiding plagiarism.

  [4.W.8] [5.W.8] [6.W.8] [7.W.8] [8.W.8]

PRIOR TO THE LESSON

- Read through the entire lesson and review the slideshow to familiarize yourself with the clinic.

- Students will be making lists of details about a topic to create their list poems.

- Consider whether or not you want to have students make their lists about a topic of classroom study. If so, have research tools available.

- Check out the bonus poems at the end of this clinic to see if any are better suited to your class as an example text than the one embedded in the clinic.

- Set up a separate surface (chart paper or white board) on which to compose a poem written collectively by you and your students.

THE LESSON

Slide 1

- Introduce the teaching poets by name (Sara and Michael) as they will appear throughout this lesson.

Slide 2

- Review the purpose of the lesson and then ask students to turn and talk about why they think lists may be important.

- Ask: Why is it important in school and in life to make lists? (Lists help us organize our thoughts and ensure that we don't forget things.)

- Ask to hear a couple student responses aloud.

Text Talk

Slide 3: "Close Call" by Sara Holbrook

- Read the poem aloud, have a student read it, and/or play the audio.

- Have students turn and talk to clarify what is happening in the poem.

- Point out that Holbrook used periods after every line.

- Ask: Is each line a complete sentence? (Yes.)

- Confirm that we do *not* need to use complete sentences in writing poetry.

Slide 4

- Ask: What does this mean: Today's poets stand on the shoulders of yesterday's giants?

- Provide a little background on Whitman.
  - He is an American poet who lived from 1819 to 1892 who was also a journalist.

Slide 5

- Provide your students with some additional background information about Whitman:
  - His major work was *Leaves of Grass*, which he self-published in 1855.
  - He is probably the most famous of all American poets.
  - He is often credited with creating the list poem, but lists have been around since workers preplanned for the pyramids.

Slide 6: "The World Below the Brine" by Walt Whitman

- Before reading the poem aloud, introduce the word *lichen* (pronounced LIKEN). A lichen is an organism, kind of like a fungus, that can live under the water or on land, clinging to rocks. For example, search "sea lichen" for images.

- Don't dwell on the unfamiliar words. A brief familiarity is all that is needed to understand the poem. If students want more info, they can research it later.

- Read the poem excerpt, have a student read it, and/or play the audio.

- Ask: What does Whitman mean by "Below the Brine"? (Under the ocean.)

- Ask: Why might this poem be considered informational text? (It contains specific details of what lives under the sea.)

- Ask: Where did he look to make this list poem? (We must assume he did first person research since photographs and videos were not available then.)

- Have students turn and talk, examining the poem in pairs to find examples of what details Whitman noticed in "The World Below the Brine."

- Note that this is simply an excerpt of this poem, chosen to reflect the poet's style, abbreviated to fit on this slide.

- If you are interested in downloading the entire poem, you can find it online: http://classiclit.about.com/library/bl-etexts/wwhitman/bl-ww-theworld .htm.

Slide 7: Text Talk: Compare the Two List Poems

- Ask: Putting these two list poems side by side, what is similar and what is different about them?

- Have students turn and talk and determine one difference between the two, in terms of either content or structure. (In Holbrook's poem, verbs play a major role. In Whitman's list poem, there are no verbs.)

- Ask them to also identify one thing that is the same between the two poems. (Both poems contain factual details without opinions or interpretations; both poems are about nature.)

- Have a couple of volunteers share their ideas aloud with the entire class.

- Point out: Both poems consist of a list of images. Holbrook's poem uses verbs; Whitman's does not. Either way is okay.

Slide 8

- Remind the writers that poetry is about the real world: what they know, what they are learning, and what they wonder about.

- Tell students that this is a picture of Michael fishing.

- Reveal that the next poem is a poem Michael wrote about a bicycle.

Slide 9

- Ask students to predict what words might go into a list poem about a bicycle.

- Collect responses. They will sound like this: *wheels, brakes, seat, handlebars, pedals,* etc.

Slide 10

- Read the poem aloud, have a student read it, and/or play the audio.

- Discuss why this poem could be considered informational text.

Work Together

Slide 11

- Choose a topic to write a list poem about with your class. Pick a person, place, or thing you will write about together. (You may wish to draw an image from your current unit of study in math, science, or social studies.)

- On a separate surface, work together as a class to create a list of details about a specific person, place, or thing.

- See what you can come up with in 2 minutes. (Check the clock and race! Eight or so details will be fine.)

- Have students rearrange this list of details to make a poem.

- Ask: Which detail would make a good first line? And then go from there.

- Look to see how your details may be rearranged for rhythm and emphasis.

- Don't spend too long on this process; you want students to see this as easily doable.

- You are simply working together to model the writing process.

Time to Write

Slide 12

- Leave your completed list poem on display so students can check in as they write.

- Time to get out a piece of paper or open writer's notebooks or computers.

- Have reference sources handy.

Slide 13

- Invite individual students to choose a topic.

- Check in with students and help them in narrowing their topics. If someone suggests "sports," for instance, help the writer narrow the topic to one sport.

- Remind students that a poem is a snapshot of life, not an entire movie.

- Make sure your class model poem is visible for review.

- Refer back to the list poems of Whitman, Holbrook, and Salinger.

Slide 14

- Note that these are just a few possibilities.

- Have the students discuss some other ideas—things they could make a list about—and turn those lists into poems of their own design.

- Have students turn and talk about ideas (for maybe a minute or so).

- Consider directing students to a particular unit of study (ancient worlds, dinosaurs, the circulatory system, etc.). Students may even take a longer text that they have written and condense it down to a list poem.

- Explain that one way to research a topic is to think carefully about it, relying on personal knowledge.
- Let students know that there are many other ways to research a topic:
  - Some writers may wish to consult a book or the Internet.
  - Other writers may find that a dictionary and thesaurus are handy tools at this point.
- Explain to students that this is like making a grocery list of detailed observations.
- Ask students to include at least eight or so details in their lists (some may come up with a lot more).

Slide 16

- Invite students to begin writing their poems, and give them the following guidelines:
  - View your lists as Legos that can be moved and stacked as you see fit.
  - Consider simply renumbering your lists until you're happy with them, and then, once you're done, recopy them.
  - Think about adding a strong introductory line and/or a concluding line.
  - Save a duplicate of your list if you're working on a computer so that the details don't get lost in the revision process.
- Circulate around the room and help students check their lists for objective facts rather than subjective opinions (*nice, yucky, interesting* are not accurate descriptors).

Share

Slide 17

- Have all of the students read their poems aloud at the same time. Students will be reading different poems but hearing their own words aloud. A seat symphony!
- Have writers share their poems with a partner.
- Have a few stand and share with the class.
- Scaffold up gradually to having students read aloud in front of the entire class.

Slide 18

- Ask: How can writing list poems help with your other writing?
- Have students turn and talk.
- Ask for some to share their ideas on how writing list poems will help them in other genres of writing. (Possible answers: Helps them organize their thoughts, be attentive to detail, and enrich their writing with facts.)

Slide 19

- Take-away: Whether it's poetry or other types of text, our writing is improved if we start with a list of facts.

Bonus Poems and Lesson Extensions

Slide 20

- These bonus poems have been selected to give you the opportunity to differentiate according to the needs of your classroom and to extend and reinforce the lesson.

Slide 21: "Skater" by Sara Holbrook

- Read the poem aloud, have a student read it, and/or play the audio.
- Ask: What details make the poem come alive? (The actions the skater makes.)
- Ask: Who is speaking in this poem? What is the point of view? (The skater; the point of view of the skater.)

Slide 22

- Have students look at the poem now that the title and the word *skate* have been covered up.
- Ask: Which details let the reader know this is not a generic sports poem, but a poem about skateboarding? (Let them identify the skater terms.)

Slide 23

- Ask: Are there opinions in this poem? (No, there are no subjective terms in the poem.) The poem is objective—it's made up of evidence, not any interpretations of the evidence.
- Ask: Does the poem attempt to persuade or tell the reader "skating is cool" or "skating is dangerous"?
- Reinforce that a list poem is a list of facts.
- Consider going back to Whitman and showing students again that he is using facts, not opinions. Explain that Whitman may have been thinking that the world below the ocean was beautiful, but that he didn't write that in the poem. Instead, his poem leads his readers to make their own interpretations.

Slide 24: "In the Deep" by Marie-Elizabeth Mali

- Next we have a list poem written from under the sea—21st century style.
- Provide some background on the poet:
  - When Marie-Elizabeth Mali is not traveling the globe in search of sea images, she resides in New York City. She is the author of *Steady,*

My Gaze (Tebot Bach, 2011) and co-editor with Annie Finch of the anthology *Villanelles* (Everyman's Library Pocket Poets, 2012). She is an avid underwater photographer. For more information please visit www.memali.com.

Slide 25

- Read through the poem, have students read it, and/or play the audio.

- Ask: Which of these sea life references are familiar to you? (Ask students to talk it over and share information—don't just define the terms for them.)

- Ask: Who is that four-limbed bubble-breather referenced in the last two lines?

- Note: Poets attempt to draw you into their world.

- Ask: How does the poem pull you in?

ASSESSMENT

Here we provide a rubric you may choose to use. We provide this as a guide knowing that you may have other goals for your class. Don't feel compelled to assess every skill mentioned in this chart. We have had more success when we zero in on a skill or two with a lesson, but we want to afford you multiple options with these clinics.

Skill	3	2	1
Relevancy	Accurately chooses compelling and descriptive facts, words, and phrases to convey an idea. Chooses the most pertinent information from his or her preliminary list for inclusion in the finished piece.	Sometimes chooses compelling and descriptive facts, words, and phrases to convey an idea. May have a detail or two included in the finished piece that is not completely supported or is not entirely relevant to the meaning of the piece.	Does not choose compelling and descriptive facts, words, and phrases to convey an idea.
Supporting Factual Details	Demonstrates the ability to research a topic using observation and multiple sources. Information presented adds to the audience's understanding of the subject matter.	Demonstrates the ability to partially research a topic using observation and multiple sources. The written piece may show a biased opinion or two.	Does not demonstrate the ability to research a topic using observation and multiple sources. No factual data is present in the writing.
Revision: Adding Transition Words and Phrases	Demonstrates an understanding of transition words and phrases and effectively uses them to make the poem coherent.	Demonstrates a basic understanding of transition words and phrases and uses them inconsistently in an attempt to make the poem coherent.	Does not demonstrate an understanding of transition words and phrases and does not strategically use them to make the poem coherent.
Close Reading	Demonstrates through classroom discussion and writing an understanding of how an author uses a list of details to support an idea.	Partially demonstrates through classroom discussion and writing an understanding of how an author uses a list of details to support an idea.	Does not demonstrate through classroom discussion and writing an understanding of how an author uses a list of details to support an idea.
Speaking Skills	Consistently demonstrates effective presentation skills using good voice projection, inflection, pacing, eye contact, and stance.	Partially demonstrates effective presentation skills using good voice projection, inflection, pacing, eye contact, and stance.	Does not demonstrate effective presentation skills using good voice projection, inflection, pacing, eye contact, and stance.
Listening Skills	Actively participates in discussions about other students' work and is tuned in to student presentations.	Occasionally participates in discussions about other students' work and is partially tuned in to student presentations.	Does not participate in discussions about other students' work and is not tuned in to student presentations.

3

The Summary Poem

What's the Big Idea?

WHY TEACH THIS?

This writing clinic will help students summarize what they have experienced, read, or learned. It will provide them with a framework, a lesson in basic narrative that will be useful in writing informational text, composing literary analysis, answering essay questions, and other types of academic writing. And since a poem is more than a straight summary, it will also lead them to relate their facts with a creative twist and provide you with an opportunity to help strengthen and assess their knowledge of poetic elements.

One of the key competencies students must master in order to strengthen their reading comprehension skills is the ability to identify the most important parts of a passage and summarize the passage accordingly. When students develop an aptitude for this, they will more easily understand the texts they encounter and will meet with more success when they are tested in this area. As they learn to find the most important details of a passage or an event, they will come to understand the importance of concise and precise writing.

This writing clinic will help students develop all of the key competencies described above. In addition, it will reinforce students' understanding of narrative structure (beginning, middle, end) while showing that these components don't necessarily have to appear in this order.

Michael: Prioritizing information is a strategy that will help our students with any reading or writing they do.

Sara: In this clinic we learn to summarize our experiences into what we call—in homage to Emily Dickinson—the *chiefest* words.

CCSS AND CORRESPONDING ANCHOR STANDARDS

- **Determine** central ideas or themes of a text and analyze their development; summarize the key supporting details and ideas.

  [4.RIT.2] [5.RIT.2] [6.RIT.2] [7.RIT.2] [8.RIT.2]

- **Determine** a theme or central idea of a text and how it is conveyed through particular details; provide a summary of the text distinct from personal opinions or judgments.

  [4.RL.2] [5.RL.2] [6.RL.2] [7.RL.2] [8.RL.2]

- **Read** and comprehend complex literary and informational texts independently and proficiently.

  [4.RL.10] [5.RL.10] [6.RL.10] [7.RL.10] [8.RL.10]

- **Integrate** and evaluate information presented in diverse media and formats, including visually, quantitatively, and orally.

  [4.SL.2] [5.SL.2] [6.SL.2] [7.SL.2] [8.SL.2]

- **Write** informative/explanatory texts to examine and convey complex ideas and information clearly and accurately through the effective selection, organization, and analysis of content.

  [4.W.2] [5.W.2] [6.W.2] [7.W.2] [8.W.2]

- **Write** narrative to develop real or imagined experiences or events using effective technique, well-chosen details, and well-structured sequences.

  [4.W.3] [5.W.3] [6.W.3] [7.W.3] [8.W.3]

- **Produce** clear and coherent writing in which the development, organization, and style are appropriate to task, purpose, and audience.

  [4.W.4] [5.W.4] [6.W.4] [7.W.4] [8.W.4]

PRIOR TO THE LESSON

- Read through the entire lesson and review the slideshow to familiarize yourself with the clinic.

- Set up a separate surface (chart paper or white board) on which to compose a poem written collectively by you and your students.

THE LESSON

Slide 1

- Introduce the teaching poets by name (Sara and Michael), as their poems will appear throughout this lesson.

Slide 2

- Review the purpose of the lesson and then ask students to turn and talk about what might be meant by a "summary poem."
- Reinforce that a narrative has a beginning, a middle, and an end.
- Consider these other possible discussion starters:
  - Ask: Does the order always have to be chronological?
  - Ask: When does summarization come in handy?

Slides 3–6

- Tell students that they are about to hear one of Sara Holbrook's shortest poems.
- Read the poem on the screen or select a reader from the class.
- Ask: This is a very short poem, but does it tell a story? (Yes.)
- Ask: What is the beginning, middle, and end of the story? (Shampoo ran into her eyes and made her cry.)
- Ask: Does it relate an experience that rings true to the reader? (It's a common experience!)

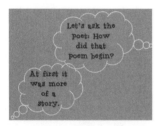

Slide 7

- This slide begins a Q and A with Sara about her writer's craft.
- Consider choosing two students to read from the slides.

Slide 8

- Note: This is a simple story that reveals a simple truth: Soap hurts the eyes!

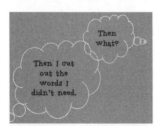

Slide 9

- Have students read from the slide as the conversation continues.

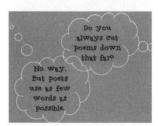

Slide 10

- Have students read from the slide as the conversation continues.

Text Talk

Slide 11

American Poet Emily Dickinson

"I hesitate which word to take, as I can take but few, and each must be the *chiefest*."

- Ask: What does Emily mean by *chiefest*? (The most important words, or the power words.)

- Ask: It's a different use of the word than we are accustomed to seeing. What does *chief* mean—and subsequently, *chiefest*? (Most important.)

- Ask students to turn and talk about something else in the world that might be labeled chiefest. (Super Bowl winner, Olympic gold medalist, Academy Award winner.)

- Give students some background information about Emily Dickinson:
  - Emily Dickinson is an American poet (December 10, 1830–May 15, 1886).
  - She is regarded as one of America's greatest poets, but she is also well known for being a bit of a hermit. Living a life of simplicity and seclusion, she wrote poetry of great power.
  - Her use of short, compact phrases set her work apart from other poets writing in her time.

Slide 12

- Discuss the two ways to pare down text:
  - **Slash and burn** (cutting out all of the words one can without losing meaning)
  - **Pick and choose** (picking out the most important words)
  - Note: Both methods lead to the same end.

- Indicate that today we are going to experiment with the *pick and choose* method.

- Let students know this is a test drive of this style of editing their own work, perhaps an approach they haven't tried before.

- Explain to students that once writers have the hang of picking out the most important words, it will be easier for them to recognize the less important words, such as articles (*a, an,* and *the*), which may be important for sentence structure but do not really add new information.

Slide 13

- See how this sixth grader is reading a story she has written and circling the most important words and phrases.

- Let students know that she is choosing words that she just can't afford to get rid of because without them her story would make no sense.

Work Together

Slide 14

- Explain: We are going to write a nonfiction narrative.
- Assure everyone that it's is going to be easy. (It is.)

Slide 15

- Ask: What is a nonfiction narrative? Can you think of some examples? (A news report, a biography, a description.)
- Ask: Where do we get our news? (Newspapers, radio, computer, speakers, or just watching the sky.)
- Explain that the next story was written by students who had recently watched images of an earthquake in Haiti. This report was typical of news reports of natural disasters.
- Explain that the students' narrative story was based on those images and on a news report on CNN that they watched together.

Slide 16

- Explain to students that they will now be learning the same sequence those students used when they were writing their narratives.
- Introduce the sequence format we will be using today for writing our narratives.
  - **Topic sentence:** A simple statement of fact
  - **Second sentence:** Another supporting statement adding more detail
  - **Unfortunately:** A third sentence beginning with the word *unfortunately*
  - **Fortunately:** A fourth sentence beginning with the word *fortunately*
  - **Finally:** A final sentence beginning with the word *finally*

Text Talk

Slide 17

- Reiterate that this story was written by students who had recently watched images of the 2010 earthquake in Haiti and heard reports of it on television. Reports were typical of an event such as this.
- Ask: Do you think it might have been difficult to come up with a *fortunately* line for the story about such a tragedy?
- Note the title of their poem: (as always) Version 1, so labeled in the expectation that changes will be made later.
- Ask: What does the word *unfortunately* do to the story? (Introduces a problem, or something bad that happens, etc.)

- Explain that this is the conflict in this narrative.
- Ask: What does the word *fortunately* do to the narrative? (Introduces something good that happens or explains how the problem is solved.)
- Explain that this is the resolution.
- Ask: What does the word *finally* do to this story? (Conclusion.)
- Explain that this story has a beginning, middle, and end.
- Ask: Could we still understand this story if we busted up the lines and read them in a different order? (Yes.)

Slide 18

- Explain that the writers then identified the most important words by underlining them.
- Ask: What makes these words important?
- Ask your students to look at which words were *not* included as the chiefest words.
- Ask them to look closely and notice how the framework words (*unfortunately, fortunately, finally*) drop away—but the remaining words still tell a story with a beginning, middle, and end.

Slide 19

- Explain that this slide illustrates the next step the students took in writing their summary poem. During this step, the words were copied over into what we call "a grocery list" of the chiefest words.
- Let students know that we also call this a poem skeleton. (See Clinic 1 for a more complete explanation of a poem skeleton if needed.)
- Explain that sometimes this Version 2 will need some connective tissue to hold it together.
- Inform students that in this final version, the students changed *recover* to *recovery* to help the poem make sense.

Work Together

Slide 20

- Lead the class through the process of writing an *unfortunately/fortunately* narrative story on a separate surface, chart paper, or a white board.
- Invite students to write about this giraffe, or give them the option of choosing a topic that relates to their current unit of study.
- Follow the framework, taking suggestions from the students as you go along.
- Entertain more than one suggestion before settling on one for each of the five lines.
- Explain that there is usually more than one good choice for each line, and tell students that you are hearing a lot of good ideas.

Time to Write

Slide 21

- Ask students to get out a sheet of paper, their writer's notebooks, or computers.
- Consider whether or not you want to have students write their nonfiction narratives about a certain subject (westward migration, coal mining, photosynthesis, percentages, etc.). If so, have research materials handy.

Slide 22

- Review the process described in the lesson for creating the narratives and the resultant summary poems. (This part will take about 15 minutes.)
- Remind students that first they are going to write their stories.
- Project Slide 20 to display the writing prompts, as needed.
- Indicate to students that when they are done, they will then choose the most important words and make a list of those words.
- Have students use this list to write their summary poems.
- When students ask why these summary poems are so amazing, tell them that it is because they convey so much information in so few words.
- Remind them of Sara's poem "Shampoo, Boo Hoo."

Slide 23

- Provide a recap for students, explaining that so far they have made two versions of their narratives:
  - Version 1 was their *unfortunately/fortunately* story.
  - Version 2 was the narrative summary poem they made after choosing the most important words.
- Explain that as they revise (Version 3, 4, 5 . . .) they may want to add more details.

Slide 24

- Suggest that perhaps they will need a Version 3 and that they will need to add or change some of the words so that their poem makes logical sense.
- Remember to reinforce the fact that they do *not* need complete sentences.

Time to Revise

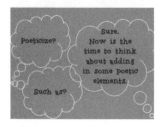

Slide 25

- Ask students to turn and talk to come up with some poetic elements.
- Allow students to come up with their own list. The discussion is important. (We provide a list on the next slide.)

Slide 26

- Your students may only know a few of these.
- Determine whether or not you would like to review some of their meanings now or leave them for a later time.

Slide 27

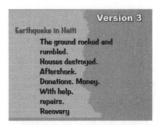

- Read through Version 3 or have a student read it.
- The next slide shows Versions 2 and 3 side by side.

Slide 28

- Ask students to turn and talk about the differences between Version 2 and Version 3.
- Ask: What poetic elements were added? (Alliteration and a close rhyme at the end.)
- Ask: Were the lines rearranged? (Yes.)
- Point out to students that one line became the title of the Version 3 poem.

Time to Revise

Slide 29

- Ask students to look back at their Version 2.
- Ask them to revise to include at least one poetic element.
- Note: You may wish to leave Slide 26 visible as they work on their revisions.

Share

Slide 30

- Have students share with a partner.
- Invite a few enthusiastic volunteers to share with the class.
- Ask students who are sharing to read more than one of their versions.
- Ask the reader: Which version is working best for you? Is there anything you still want to change? (This gives the rest of the class the opportunity to hear the poet's thinking.)
- Keep in mind that if you chose to have students write about specific subject matter, you may see opportunities to reinforce the associated content area learning as they read their pieces aloud.

Slide 31

- Reiterate that narratives may be fiction or nonfiction.
- Remind writers that poems do not need to contain complete sentences.
- Review the idea that poems can be informational text when we base them on real facts.
- Provide a recap for students that during revision we are able to add poetic elements into our narrative poem.

Bonus Poems and Lesson Extensions

Slide 32

- These bonus poems have been selected to give you the opportunity to differentiate the needs of your classroom.

Slide 33: "Racing With Risk" by Sara Holbrook

- Note that "Racing With Risk" is a narrative summary poem.
- Read through the two slides (it just wouldn't fit on one slide), have a student read them, and/or play the audio (on the next slide).

Slide 34

- Poet Sara Holbrook says, "This narrative poem is based on a true eyeball chat I once had with a squirrel. Writing the poem took much longer than that squirrel and I spent looking at one another. I had to write the poem and then trim it down, just as you did in your short narratives."
- Ask: What is happening in this narrative poem? (The narrator is talking to a squirrel.)
- Ask: Do you think this poem is fiction or nonfiction? (Nonfiction.)
- Ask students to identify the narrative elements in the poem. (Beginning, middle, end.)
- To find a compare/contrast opportunity, go to the next slide.

Slide 35: "Poem" by Emily Dickinson

- Read the poem aloud, have a student read it, and/or play the audio (on the next slide).
- Ask: What is happening in this poem? (A bird is just walking along.)
- Provide students with some background information on this poem by Emily Dickinson:
  - Emily Dickinson (1830–1886) did not title her poems.
  - This one was first published in 1891, 5 years after her death, under the title of "In the Garden." It also appears in her complete works as Poem 328.

Slide 36

- Ask: What happens at the end of the story?

- Clarify for students that "plashless" means splashing without a sound.

- Ask students to compare/contrast this poem with Sara's.

- Ask them something like this: What is one thing that is similar? One that is different? (Entertain lots of ideas—there is no single right or wrong answer.)

Slide 37: "My Life as a Veggie Zombie" by Steve Swinburne

- Read the poem aloud, have a student read it, and/or play the audio.

- This poem is just plain fun.

- Ask: What's the story here? What's happening? (The zombie is digging through the fridge for veggies.)

- Ask: Steve staggers in and out of rhyme like a true zombie. Can you find examples? (Have students turn and talk.)

- Ask: Which do you think is more important to the poem: the story or the rhyme pattern? (The story; the pattern supports the story.)

- Provide students with some background information about Steve Swinburne:

  ○ Steve Swinburne is the author of many nonfiction books for kids, a zombie aficionado, and a ukulele maestro.

  ○ More about Steve, his books, and school visits can be found at www .steveswinburne.com.

Slides 38–39: "Don't You Boys Know Any Nice Songs?" by Michael Salinger

- Tell students you will now prove to them that all narrative poems . . .

  ○ don't have to rhyme.

  ○ aren't about nature.

- Ask: What is the setting of this narrative?

- Let students know that this is a poem by Michael Salinger, reflecting on his time playing in a rock band.

- Ask: How does the story end? (The boys have to stop playing, but not until they start to sound like a real band.)

- Mention to students, as a postscript, that the skinny fellow in the black jeans is Michael Salinger.

ASSESSMENT

Here we provide a rubric you may choose to use. We provide this as a guide knowing that you may have other goals for your class. Don't feel compelled to assess every skill mentioned in this chart. We have had more success when we zero in on a skill or two with a lesson, but we want to afford you multiple options with these clinics.

Skill	3	2	1
Content Knowledge	Demonstrates an understanding of content area information and is able to identify the main idea.	Demonstrates some understanding of content area information and is able to identify the main idea. May include one or two details that are not pertinent to the main theme of the piece.	Includes inaccuracies when writing about content area information and is not able to identify the main idea.
Narrative Structure	Consistently and accurately develops a narrative story using the prescribed pattern.	Partially develops a narrative story using the prescribed pattern. Perhaps a line does not reflect its prompt or is irrelevant to the narrative.	Does not develop a narrative story using the prescribed pattern.
Revision	Effectively condenses writing into a summary poem by choosing the most powerful words and eliminating unnecessary language.	Partially condenses writing by choosing the most powerful words and eliminating unnecessary language. Finished piece may still show room to be even more precise and concise.	Does not condense writing by choosing the most powerful words and eliminating unnecessary language.
Speaking Skills	Consistently demonstrates effective presentation skills using good voice projection, inflection, pacing, eye contact, and stance.	Partially demonstrates effective presentation skills using good voice projection, inflection, pacing, eye contact, and stance.	Does not demonstrate effective presentation skills using good voice projection, inflection, pacing, eye contact, and stance.
Listening Skills	Actively participates in discussions about other students' work and is tuned in to student presentations.	Occasionally participates in discussions about other students' work and is tuned in to student presentations.	Does not participate in discussions about other students' work and is not tuned in to student presentations.

4

The Found Poem

Finding the Unusual in the Usual

WHY TEACH THIS?

In a manner of speaking, all poems are found poems. There is no such thing as a signed, sealed, delivered poem. We have to go looking for them.

This lesson is designed to get students to examine and analyze their surroundings and/or a piece of text. It is intended to give students pause. We want to raise students' awareness of the words swirling around them, waiting to be found.

In writing a *found poem*, we must first identify key words that may be used to describe a person, place, or event. For our models, we gathered words from a hardware store, an article on Abraham Lincoln's death, and a collection of flash cards about the digestive system. You will find two lessons based on the found poem model in this clinic, with the second part beginning on Slide 15.

Being able to pause and closely analyze text in order to identify key words is a reading skill that will benefit all students in all content areas. Through using this skill, student writers will develop a deeper understanding of the text they are analyzing and be able to see the authentic benefits of implementing strong, image-evoking language in their own writing.

Michael: This is what we mean when we talk about looking at the world through a poet's eye.

Sara: Developing a poet's eye means cultivating an eye for detail.

CCSS AND CORRESPONDING ANCHOR STANDARDS

- **Read** closely to determine what the text says explicitly and to make logical inferences from it; cite specific textual evidence when writing to speaking to support conclusions drawn from the text.

  [4.RL.1] [5.RL.1] [6.RL.1] [7.RL.1] [8.RL.1]

- **Determine** a theme or central idea of a text and how it is conveyed through particular details; provide a summary of the text distinct from personal opinions or judgments.

  [4.RL.2] [5.RL.2] [6.RL.2] [7.RL.2] [8.RL.2]

- **Interpret** words and phrases as they are used in a text, including determining technical, connotative, and figurative meanings, and analyze how specific word choices shape meaning or tone.

  [4.RL.4] [5.RL.4] [6.RL.4] [7.RL.4] [8.RL.4]

- **Demonstrate** understanding of word relationships and nuances in word meanings.

  [4.L.5] [5.L.5] [6.L.5] [7.L.5] [8.L.5]

- **Read** and comprehend complex literary and informational texts independently and proficiently.

  [4.RL.10] [5.RL.10] [6.RL.10] [7.RL.10] [8.RL.10]

- **Interpret** words and phrases as they are used in a text, including determining technical, connotative, and figurative meanings, and analyze how specific word choices shape meaning or tone.

  [4.RIT.4] [5.RIT.4] [6.RIT.4] [7.RIT.4] [8.RIT.4]

- **Write** informative/explanatory texts to examine and convey complex ideas and information clearly and accurately through the effective selection, organization, and analysis of content.

  [4.W.3] [5.W.3] [6.W.3] [7.W.3] [8.W.3]

- **Write** narrative to develop real or imagined experiences or events using effective technique, well-chosen details, and well-structured sequences.

  [4.W.2] [5.W.2] [6.W.2] [7.W.2] [8.W.2]

- **Produce** clear and coherent writing in which the development, organization, and style are appropriate to task, purpose, and audience.

  [4.W.4] [5.W.4] [6.W.4] [7.W.4] [8.W.4]

PRIOR TO THE LESSON

- Read through the entire lesson and review the slideshow to familiarize yourself with the clinic.

- Check out the bonus poems at the end of this clinic. One may be better suited for a model poem for your class than the one embedded in the clinic. Select the poem that works best for you and your students—this is your choice.

- Note that students will be making lists of details about a topic to create their found poems.

  o Students will be examining a real-life setting or an event and identifying key words to form a poem.

  o And/or students will be analyzing a block of text and identifying key words to make into a poem.

- Identify in advance what you want your students to observe and/or where you want them to find a block of text to work with.

- Note that nonfiction or fiction will work just as well.

- Set up a separate surface (chart paper or white board) on which to compose a poem written collectively by you and your students.

- Have markers available for Part 2 of the writing clinic.

- Consider dividing this lesson into two sessions:
  - A poem found in a specific place
  - A poem found in a block of text

THE LESSON

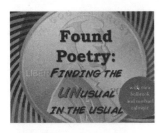

Slide 1

- Introduce the teaching poets by name (Sara and Michael) as they will appear throughout this lesson.

Slides 2–3

- Introduce the *found poem* as a fun poetic form, especially for those who say, "I'm no poet."

- Tell students that writing a found poem is a little like finding forgotten money in your pocket. You weren't really looking for it, but there it is!

- Announce that first we are going to do a word gather; just look around and see what words can be found, and then use them to make a poem.

- Let students know that they also will be analyzing a piece of text to identify key words and then using them to form a poem.

Slides 4–6: Found Poetry Defined

- Explain that a found poem happens when you arrange words you just found somewhere into a poem.

- Where do you find these words?

- Just about anywhere.

Slide 7

- Get students started by asking them to identify some places where words can be found.

- Here are some places. Can they think of others?

- Ask students to confer with each other for 30 seconds to come up with some more places to go looking for words. (Other places at school, at home, in the grocery store, on street signs—any place there is text.)

Slides 8–9

- Explain that Michael isn't just a poet; he's a regular person.

- People get weird ideas about poets—they think that they live in meadows and stroll along beaches all the time.

- Not true. Poets are regular people whose faucets break and doors need repair.

- Explain that Michael once found a poem at the local hardware store.

Slide 10

- Introduce Debbie, from Sara and Michael's local hardware store. (She is not as dangerous as she looks with that hammer in her hand.)

- Ask students to examine this picture to see what words they can see.

- Invite students to get out of their seats to take a look.

- Tell students that there is no need to write the words down—they should just see how many words they can find.

- Let them know that the words don't have to be in print. For instance, there are funnels on the bottom shelf. *Funnel* also counts as a found word.

Text Talk

Slide 11: "Hardware Store" by Michael Salinger

- Read the poem aloud, have a student read it, and/or play the audio.

- This is a fun one to read again. Try this for a second reading:
  - Divide the class in half.
  - Ask one half to read the first column (six *hammers* and one *drill*)
  - You read the center column.
  - Have the other half of the class read the third column (five *do its* and one *yourself*).

Work Together

Slide 12: The Classroom Found Poem

- Classrooms are busy places. Words on the wall. Words on shirts. Words on books.

- Ask students to take a minute to look around the room and find words.

- Collect these words on a separate surface.

- Ask students to come to the classroom writing space (whiteboard, etc.) and write the words themselves. (You can also write them yourself, but it's more fun to have students do it.)

- Give the class about 3–5 minutes to collect the words.

- Discuss how these words might be arranged to make a poem.

- Explain: You do not need to use every word collected in your poem. Some you may wish to use once, and some you may wish to repeat.

- Remind them how Michael played with the words from the hardware store in his poem.

- Draft a quick poem out of the found words as students offer their ideas.

- Remember that there is no need to spend too much time on this. You simply want to model the writing process before sending students out to collect words for their own found poems.

Time to Write

Slide 13

- Consider taking a field trip to the cafeteria, library, or even a local park for writers to gather words in order to create their own found poem.

- Keep in mind that there are usually plenty of words on the hallway walls of every school.

- Consider assigning this as homework and ask students to gather words on the bus ride home, from the stuff under their beds, in the family junk drawer, etc.

- Ask the students to take all of their gathered-up words and start to poeticize!

- Ask students how they can use repeated sounds, rhythms, rhymes.

- Twist and turn the phrases with your students to come up with something surprising, out of the ordinary.

Share

Slide 14

- Designate class time for your writers to share. This applies whether or not the found poems are composed in class or at home.

- Have students first share with a partner, and then have them share with the class.

Part 2

Slide 15: Part 2: How to Create a Found Poem From a Piece of Nonfiction Text

- Ask the class to name other sources of nonfiction text. (Encyclopedias, journals, instruction manuals, the school handbook.)

Slide 16: *Harper's Weekly*

- Provide students with some background information about this publication:
  - *Harper's Weekly* was distributed from 1857 until 1916.
  - It was a weekly newspaper.
- Ask if students can name a weekly publication that might be published today. (*Time*, *People*, the local arts and events newspapers.)

Text Talk

Slide 17: *Harper's Weekly* Article About Lincoln's Death

- Explain to your students that this report appeared 11 days after Lincoln's assassination.
- Read aloud or have a student read through the text.
- Let your students know that Sara has written a poem that she found in this text and that you are going to work together to see if the class can predict a few of the words and phrases she might have chosen.
- Ask the class to work together to analyze and identify key words in the text and see if they can predict which words Sara selected for her found poem.
- As you read the text, pause after every few lines so that students can call out key words and short phrases.

Slide 18

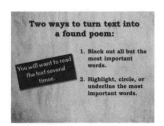

- Explain to students that after they have analyzed the text a bit, they are ready to find the words for a poem.
- Give them these two options for how this can be done:
  - Black out all the words we do not want, leaving the key words visible.
  - Underline or highlight the key words.
- Note: This echoes the *slash and burn* or *pick and choose* techniques discussed in the Summary Poem writing clinic, Clinic 3.

Slide 19

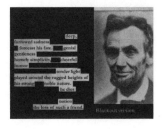

- Explain to students that this is a model of a blackout approach to finding a poem in the article.
- Let students know that identifying the key words is a mixture of personal choice and logic.
- Inform students that in this particular case, Sara did the choosing. Tell them that other readers might make different choices.
- Reveal that the chosen words are the same in both Slides 19 and 20.
- Warn students that if they want to take the blackout approach, they should underline the words they want to keep before they rip into the text with a permanent black marker.
- Remind students that in all cases, it is important *not* to destroy original source documents unless you (the teacher) have deemed them to be disposable.

Slide 20

- This is a model of highlighted text.
- Ask students which approach they would prefer to take: highlight or blackout.
- Note that the blackout version can almost look like a piece of artwork.

Slide 21

- Note that this is a found poem from the *Harper's Weekly* article, found and arranged by Sara.
- Read the poem aloud, have a student read it, and/or play the audio.
- Ask: Does the found poem completely summarize everything from the article? (No.)
- Ask: What kinds of words were *not* chosen? (Articles, passive verbs, etc.)
- Show students how Sara changed the words slightly in the last lines so that they would make sense in the context of the poem. (*Loss* to *loses*, inserts *the*.)
- Point out to students that this entire phrase was not chosen: "are now seen to have been but." Ask: Why not? (Not powerful words.)

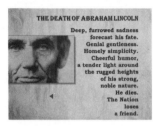

Slide 22

- Reinforce that no antique newspapers were harmed in the making of this found poem.
- Explain that, likewise, students are not to damage library books or magazines or their birth certificates. First, make a copy and then mark that up!

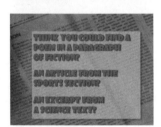

Slide 23

- Discuss where students might look for text for their found poem.
- You may wish to guide them to a particular book or specific subject matter. (Students may copy the text and work from that.) Consider these additional possibilities:
  - Cutting up old magazines can be fun.
  - Scanning the text and doing the highlighting or blacking out on a computer is a green option.

Time to Write

Slide 24

- Have students get out a sheet of paper or their writer's notebooks.
- Make certain each student has identified a block of text and that it is safe to mark on it.

- Note: A paragraph or two is usually plenty of text to work with.

- Have markers available for the highlighting or blacking-out process.

- Ask students to note the following information for their found text: date of publication, publisher, and author. They will need this information in order to include a citation with their final poem.

Share

Slide 25

- Designate class time for your writers to share. This applies whether or not the found poems are composed in class or at home.

- Have students first share with a partner, then have them share with the class.

- Ask students to cite the source of the article and indicate why they chose that piece of text.

Slide 26: Take Away

- Look around. There is poetry waiting to be found!

Bonus Poems and Lesson Extensions

Slide 27

- These bonus poems have been selected to give you the opportunity to differentiate according to the needs of your classroom and to extend and reinforce the lesson.

Slide 28: "Weekday Morning Haiku" by Sara Holbrook

- Sara Holbrook says, "Every morning in our house the dog erupts in fury at (you guessed it) the mailman."

- Explain to students that this is a found poem she got by just listening and looking.

Slide 29: "Find a Poem" by Georgia Heard

- Read the poem aloud, have a student read it, and/or play the audio.

- Have fun with this poem: Invite several students to read, taking turns.

- Consider using this as a mentor text for having students write their own poems found in a thesaurus.

- Familiarize students with the poet.
  - ○ Georgia Heard is an esteemed poet, author, and educator who lives in Florida and travels the world speaking about and through poetry. "Find a Poem" is from her book *The Arrow Finds Its Mark* (Roaring Brook Press, 2012), a rich resource for found poems.
  - ○ More information about Georgia Heard can be found at www .georgiaheard.com.

Slide 30

- Poet Michael Salinger says, "I found this poem in a set of flash cards about the digestive system . . .
  - ○ And then I added a few of my own . . .
  - ○ That's okay. We make our own rules in this poetry thing . . .
  - ○ I took this picture in the marketplace in Marrakesh, Morocco."

ASSESSMENT

Here we provide a rubric you may choose to use. We provide this as a guide knowing that you may have other goals for your class. Don't feel compelled to assess every skill mentioned in this chart. We have had more success when we zero in on a skill or two with a lesson, but we want to afford you multiple options with these clinics.

Skill	3	2	1
Careful Reading	Demonstrates the ability to determine the theme or central idea of a text and understand how it is conveyed through particular details.	Partially demonstrates the ability to determine the theme or central idea of a text and understand how it is conveyed through particular details.	Does not demonstrate the ability to determine the theme or central idea of a text and understand how it is conveyed through particular details.
Word Meaning	Demonstrates knowledge of the technical, connotative, and figurative meanings of words and phrases as they are used in the text. Analyzes how specific word choices shape meaning or tone.	Partially demonstrates knowledge of the technical, connotative, and figurative meanings of words and phrases as they are used in the text. Partially analyzes how specific word choices shape meaning or tone. May miss an important detail when selecting the most important words.	Does not demonstrate knowledge of the technical, connotative, and figurative meanings of words and phrases as they are used in the text. Is unable to analyze how specific word choices shape meaning or tone.
Relevant Content	Effectively selects terms from a particular text or research that are informative and that convey relevant ideas, concepts, and information.	Partially selects terms from a particular text or research that are informative and that convey relevant ideas, concepts, and information. May include an extraneous idea or fail to connect the selected ideas with smooth transitions.	Does not select terms from a particular text or research that are informative and that convey relevant ideas, concepts, and information.
Speaking Skills	Consistently demonstrates effective presentation skills using good voice projection, inflection, pacing, eye contact, and stance.	Partially demonstrates effective presentation skills using good voice projection, inflection, pacing, eye contact, and stance.	Does not demonstrate effective presentation skills using good voice projection, inflection, pacing, eye contact, and stance.
Listening Skills	Actively participates in discussions about other students' work and is tuned in to student presentations.	Occasionally participates in discussions about other students' work and is tuned in to student presentations.	Does not participate in discussions about other students' work and is not tuned in to student presentations.

5

Feelings Made Visual

WHY TEACH THIS?

Show, don't tell.

We've heard it a bazillion times and said it a gazillion more.

But how does that really work? It means using visual language to describe an event, person, place, or thing in a way that the reader can picture what's going on. Take the *s* off of *show* and what word do you have? *How*. If we are showing rather than telling, we are describing *how* something works.

In this clinic we will rewrite a simple poem using mentor text. This exercise will have the writers "try on" a feeling, noting what physical response they might logically have to an emotion. This will help students convey what they have experienced, imagined, thought, and felt in their future writing.

The mentor text in this clinic contains a strong concluding couplet that sums up the entire poem. This will give you an opportunity to show students how effective a strong conclusion can be in any piece of writing. Of course, not all poems have a strong conclusion, but this particular poem does.

There is also a reference to the proper use of gerunds, which is often an area of confusion for many learning English as an additional language. You may use this to reinforce your teaching of grammar conventions. Science teachers may also want to use this clinic as part of a unit on drug abuse prevention.

Sara: As a former community education specialist for the National Council on Alcohol and Drug Abuse, I learned that we need to foster an understanding in kids that feelings come and go—the good, the bad, and the very ugly. Embracing this can help us have a healthy outlook on life.

Michael: Teachers are often up against some pretty slick advertising messages telling kids to "take this and you'll feel better," which leads kids to think that feelings need to be muted or medicated away, and that can lead to dangerous lifestyles.

As a writing instructor you can use this clinic as a touchstone, referring back to it and reminding and encouraging students to use visual language in their stories and essays as you confer with them about their more complex pieces of text.

CCSS AND CORRESPONDING ANCHOR STANDARDS

- **Demonstrate** understanding of figurative language, word relationships, and nuances in word meanings.

  [4.L.5] [5.L.5] [6.L.5] [7.L.5] [8.L.5]

- **Interpret** words and phrases as they are used in a text, including determining technical, connotative, and figurative meanings, and analyze how specific word choices shape meaning or tone.

  [4.RL.4] [5.RL.4] [6.RL.4] [7.RL.4] [8.RL.4]

- **Analyze** the structure of texts, including how specific sentences, paragraphs, and larger portions of the text (e.g., a section, a chapter, scene, or stanza) relate to each other and the whole.

  [4.RL.5] [5.RL.5] [6.RL.5] [7.RL.5] [8.RL.5]

- **Read** and comprehend complex literary and informational texts independently and proficiently.

  [4.RL.10] [5.RL.10] [6.RL.10] [7.RL.10] [8.RL.10]

- **Write** informative/explanatory texts to examine and convey complex ideas and information clearly and accurately through the effective selection, organization, and analysis of content.

  [4.W.2] [5.W.2] [6.W.2] [7.W.2] [8.W.2]

- **Write** narrative to develop real or imagined experiences or events using effective technique, well-chosen details, and well-structured sequences.

  [4.W.3] [5.W.3] [6.W.3] [7.W.3] [8.W.3]

- **Produce** clear and coherent writing in which the development, organization, and style are appropriate to task, purpose, and audience.

  [4.W.4] [5.W.4] [6.W.4] [7.W.4] [8.W.4]

- **Demonstrate** command of the conventions of Standard English grammar and usage when writing or speaking.

  [4.L.1] [5.L.1] [6.L.1] [7.L.1] [8.L.1]

PRIOR TO THE LESSON

- Read through the entire lesson and review the slideshow to familiarize yourself with the clinic.

- Note that one of the bonus poems at the end of this clinic may be better suited to use as a model for your class than the one embedded in the clinic. Select the poem that works best for you and your students—your choice.

- Set up a separate surface (chart paper or white board) on which to compose a poem written collectively by you and your students.

THE LESSON

Slide 1

- Introduce the teaching poets by name (Sara and Michael), as they will appear throughout this clinic.

Slide 2

- Emphasize that though we are going to write a poem in this lesson, using visuals to describe feelings is something that writers also do in prose and nonfiction writing.

Slide 3

- Ask: How many of you have had a teacher say to you, "Show, don't tell"?
- Ask: What do you think that really means?
- Ask: What would happen to this word *show* if we took away the *s*?
- See the next slide for an example.

Slide 4

- Explain to students that when we show and don't tell, we describe *how* something happens.
- Tell students that today we are going to describe *how* feelings really feel.

Slide 5

- Ask: Have you ever felt like this image?
- Have students turn and talk about the last time they were angry and one thing that they did. (Have them talk about what they did with their hands, their feet, their eyebrows—their physical reactions to the emotion.)
- Note that this discussion is not about what made them angry, but rather it's about how they physically reacted to the emotion.
- Ask the students to tell you what instructions they would give someone who wanted to look angry.

Text Talk

Slide 6: "Angry Me" by Sara Holbrook

- Read the poem aloud, have a student read it, and/or play the audio. Note: The poem has been reformatted into two columns to fit on the slide.

- Ask students to identify the pattern of the poem.

- Ask if any of the actions that Sara describes in the poem are ones that they heard or mentioned in their turn-and-talk.

- Note that this will become the mentor text for students as they use visual language to describe a feeling through poetry.

Slide 7

- Analyzing the structure of the poem "Angry Me."

- Note: There is also a rhyme pattern in this poem.

- Make it clear to students that when they use this as a mentor text for their own writing, they do not need to rhyme until they get to the last two lines. There are a couple of benefits to this:

  ○ For students who are dying to rhyme, this gives them that opportunity.

  ○ For students who get hung up on rhymes, this limits them to the last two lines.

Slide 8

- Analyze the conclusion of the poem.

- Review quickly what a couplet is (two lines with end rhymes).

- Note that the last stanza breaks the pattern of the poem.

- Explain that any time writers build a pattern and then break that pattern, it really gets the reader's attention.

Slide 9

- Note: For second language learners, when to add "ing" to a verb can be confusing.

- Consider the makeup of your class and determine whether or not you want to go into this and the next two slides in detail.

Slide 10

- Note that today we are going to write in present tense, without a preceding verb.

Slide 11

- This slide gives you the opportunity to reteach the term *gerund*.

Work Together

Slide 12

- Introduce the idea that you and the class are going to change the title of the "Angry Me" poem to reflect a different emotion and then you're going to rewrite the poem.

Slide 13

- Ask: What does it mean to feel *weird*? (Note the variance of the responses.)
- Ask: Is it true that *weird* can mean a lot of different things? (This is the point—*weird* can mean so many different things; it actually means nothing.)

Slides 14–15

- Explain to students that descriptive language may include references to all of the senses as well as to actions.

Slide 16

- Encourage everyone in the class to "try on" feeling weird.
- Have students stand next to their desks and act out feeling weird.
- Tell them to remember what they are physically doing and what they see others physically doing.
- Explain that these observations are research for their writing.

Work Together

Slide 17

- On a separate surface (chart paper or white board), lead the students in composing a group poem.
- Consider jumping back to Slide 6 for a quick review of the mentor text.
- Explain to students that this poem that they write together will become the model for them when they write independently.

Time to Write

Slide 18

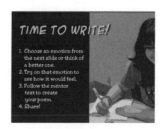

- Have students get out a piece of paper or their writer's notebooks.
- Discuss the writing process:
  - Choose an emotion from the next slide or think of a better one.
  - Try on that emotion to see how it would feel.
  - Follow the mentor text to create your poem. (Either leave the poem you wrote together as a class on display for the students or put up Slide 6.)
- Share!

Slide 19

- Affirm that students may use one of these emotions or they may choose another.
- Explain: This list is to get you started, not to hold you back.
- Check in and make sure that the writers are on the right track if they chose their own word.
- Make sure that no one has chosen an inappropriate word such as *retarded* or *spastic*.

Slide 20

- Explain that not all poems have a strong conclusion, but our mentor text does.
- Inform students that a creative summary stanza is key to making the poem work.
- Ask: What are some alternatives to "the worst thing is"?
  - The best thing is
  - The sweetest thing is
  - The most dangerous thing is
  - This list is endless. Just entertain a few suggestions and move on with the writing.

Slide 21

- Explain that all genres of writing are enriched by a strong conclusion.
- Remember, a couplet consists of two lines with end rhymes. For more on couplets, see Clinic 6.

Share

Slide 22

- Have students share with a partner and then take turns sharing with the class.
- Note that these are good pieces for students to use as they practice reading with expression.
- Point out a line or two you found particularly effective or creative after each student's presentation.
- Note particularly strong conclusions.

Slide 23

- Explain to students that sensory language can be used in all of their writing to describe feelings.
- Remind students that a strong conclusion summarizes what has gone before.
- Tell students that adding "ing" to a verb means that the action is ongoing.

Bonus Poems and Lesson Extensions

Slide 24

- These bonus poems have been selected to give you the opportunity to differentiate according to the needs of your classroom and to extend and reinforce the lesson.

Slide 25: "The Blues for Kids" by Sharon Draper

- Read the poem aloud, have a student read it, and/or play the audio (on the next slide).

Slide 26

- Ask: How does Sharon use comparisons to describe what she means by "the blues"?
- Ask: What does she mean "if we didn't have blue, we couldn't see the stars"? (Blue is a backdrop for glittering stars.)
- Ask: How does she show that having the blues is not all bad? (She draws positive comparisons to things that are blue.)
- Provide background on author Sharon Draper:

- She is a *New York Times* best-selling children's and young adult author, a former teacher, and teacher of the year. She is the recipient of numerous awards for her writing. For more information about Sharon and her stellar books, visit www.sharondraper.com.

Slide 27: "Hungry" by Michael Salinger

- Read the poem aloud, have a student read it, and/or play the audio.
- Ask: What is the pattern that Michael Salinger used to compose this poem? (It is the same pattern as Sara Holbrook's "Angry Me" poem.)
- This is a fun poem to act out!

Slide 28: "Feelings Make Me Real" by Sara Holbrook

- Explain that accepting our feelings as valid and (most often) transient is healthy for us.
- Note that this poem may be an impetus for further discussion about the benefits of writing about feelings rather than acting them out or trying to medicate them away with drugs.

ASSESSMENT

Here we provide a rubric you may choose to use. We provide this as a guide knowing that you may have other goals for your class. Don't feel compelled to assess every skill mentioned in this chart. We have had more success when we zero in on a skill or two with a lesson, but we want to afford you multiple options with these clinics.

Skill	3	2	1
Careful Reading	Demonstrates, through classroom discussion and writing, an understanding of the impact of word choice on meaning and tone.	Partially demonstrates, through classroom discussion and writing, an understanding of the impact of word choice on meaning and tone. May include a single detail in the final piece that may not seem relevant to the piece.	Does not demonstrate, through classroom discussion and writing, an understanding of the impact of word choice on meaning and tone.
Structure and Organization	Demonstrates the ability to recognize and re-create a writing structure, such as a strong conclusion.	Partially demonstrates the ability to recognize and re-create a writing structure, such as a strong conclusion. May make a single comparison that may not seem logical or may not be backed by objective observations.	Does not demonstrate the ability to recognize and re-create a writing structure, such as a strong conclusion.
Grammar Conventions	Demonstrates an understanding of how to use nouns and gerund verbs in the analysis and writing of poetry.	Partially demonstrates an understanding of how to use nouns and gerund verbs in the analysis and writing of poetry. May make a minor grammatical error.	Does not demonstrate an understanding of how to use nouns and gerund verbs in the analysis and writing of poetry.
Connotative Word Meaning	Demonstrates an understanding of connotative word meanings when using visual language to describe a feeling.	Occasionally demonstrates an understanding of the connotative word meanings when using visual language to describe a feeling. May make a comparison that does not seem logical or is not backed by objective evidence.	Does not demonstrate an understanding of connotative word meanings when using visual language to describe a feeling.
Speaking Skills	Consistently demonstrates effective presentation skills using good voice projection, inflection, pacing, eye contact, and stance.	Partially demonstrates effective presentation skills using good voice projection, inflection, pacing, eye contact, and stance.	Does not demonstrate effective presentation skills using good voice projection, inflection, pacing, eye contact, and stance.
Listening Skills	Actively participates in discussions about other students' work and is tuned in to student presentations.	Occasionally participates in discussions about other students' work and is tuned in to student presentations.	Does not participate in discussions about other students' work and is not tuned in to student presentations.

6

Couplets on the Brain

WHY TEACH THIS?

A couplet just may be the simplest form of poetry. But, like cornerstones, couplets support more sophisticated forms of poetry such as sonnets, quatrains, and the poetry that resides within Shakespeare's plays. They appear in advertising jingles (*Plop plop, fizz fizz, Oh what a relief it is*), jury summations (*If the glove does not fit, you must acquit*), and well-known adages (*A stitch in time saves nine*).

Rhyme helps us remember grammar rules—*When two vowels go walking, the first one does the talking*—and forecasts the weather—*Red at night, shepherd's delight, red in the morning, shepherds take warning*. Couplets are all around us, so why not put them to work in the classroom?

In this clinic, we will write couplets with our students and then they will write on their own as they take subject matter from their imagination and then from their content area learning and fit them into memorable couplets. We will then stack some of these couplets up as we build a longer piece.

Sara: I confess: I love couplets. They are fun and memorable. And I like to play with them.

Michael: While I do not use end rhyme a whole lot, I appreciate it when it is done well (done well being the key component).

CCSS AND CORRESPONDING ANCHOR STANDARDS

- **Demonstrate** understanding of figurative language, word relationships, and nuances in word meanings.

  [4.L.5] [5.L.5] [6.L.5] [7.L.5] [8.L.5]

- **Analyze** the structure of texts, including how specific sentences, paragraphs, and larger portions of the text (e.g., a section, chapter, scene, or stanza) relate to each other and the whole.

  [4.RL.5] [5.RL.5] [6.RL.5] [7.RL.5] [8.RL.5]

- **Read** and comprehend complex literary and informational texts independently and proficiently.

    [4.RL.10] [5.RL.10] [6.RL.10] [7.RL.10] [8.RL.10]

- **Write** informative/explanatory texts to examine and convey complex ideas and information clearly and accurately through the effective selection, organization, and analysis of content.

    [4.W.2] [5.W.2] [6.W.2] [7.W.2] [8.W.2]

- **Produce** clear and coherent writing in which the development, organization, and style are appropriate to task, purpose, and audience.

    [4.W.4] [5.W.4] [6.W.4] [7.W.4] [8.W.4]

- **Conduct** short as well as more sustained research projects based on focused questions, demonstrating understanding of the subject under investigation.

    [4.W.7] [5.W.7] [6.W.7] [7.W.7] [8.W.7]

PRIOR TO THE LESSON

- Read through the entire lesson and review the slideshow to familiarize yourself with the clinic.

- Note that one of the bonus poems at the end of this clinic may be better suited to use as a model for your class than the one embedded in the clinic. Select the poem that works best for you and your students—your choice.

- Set up a separate surface (chart paper or white board) on which to compose a poem written collectively by you and your students.

THE LESSON

Slide 1

- Introduce the teaching poets by name (Sara and Michael), as they will appear throughout this lesson.

Slide 2

- Ask: What are we going to learn today?

- Explain to students that they will be learning about couplets, which are fun and easy to create.

- Reinforce that this is going to be as fun as (well) a couple of monkeys.

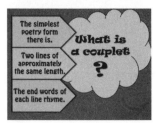

Slide 3

- Ask students to turn and talk for 30 seconds to come up with a definition of what they believe a couplet to be.

Slide 4

- Couplets are so easy; it's almost silly to have to define them. But here is a definition anyway!

- Explain that couplets are the simplest poetry form there is. They are made up of two lines of approximately the same length, and the end words of each line rhyme.

- Ask students if they can think of a couplet off the top of their heads. (*I before E, except after C*, for instance.)

Slide 5

- Share this mnemonic device with your students.

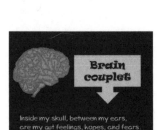

Text Talk

Slide 6

- Read the sample couplet aloud, or have a student read it.
- Ask: What makes this a couplet? (Two lines, one rhyme.)

Slide 7

- Explain that there is one problem with couplets.
- You may be encountering this problem already!

Slide 8

- Couplets are fun. Plain and simple.

Slide 9

- Explain that couplets are the components of sonnets, quatrains, and other more complex types of poetry.

- Note that as students come to understand and create couplets, they will move beyond just creating a rhyming word group (*a cat sat flat on a mat and that is that*).

Slide 10: "My Bossy Brain" by Sara Holbrook

- Read the poem aloud, have a student read it, and/or play the audio.

- Ask students if they can identify the couplets in this poem.

- Ask: What happens in the last verse? (The pattern changes.)

Slide 11

- Explain that poetry is a wonderful place for students to experiment with patterns and changing patterns, because poems are short and the rules are flexible.

- Remind students that, just as with our other writing, in poetry we never want any of our writing to be too predictable.

Slide 12

- Explain that changing a pattern is a powerful tool for a writer.

- Emphasize to students that it is important to be purposeful in our changes, so we don't look like we just missed a beat.

Slide 13

- Rhyme for kids is both a blessing and a curse.

- Rhyme is fun and engaging for kids to read and write.

- Remind students that rhyme is terribly tedious when it is used too frequently or forced, or if it takes the main stage, leaving imagery and details in the wings.

- It is not fair to introduce poetry to students through the use of nursery rhymes and then continue on to sonnets without letting them experiment with rhyme in their own writing.

- Note that using rhyme is like riding a bucking bronco—you have to hold the reins tightly or you wind up in the dust.

Slide 14

- Rhyme *is* easy.

- Rhyme is also memorable.

- But the important thing to remember is: *Rhyme by itself is never enough.*

Slide 15

- Ask: What are some ways that poetry can create meaning for the reader? (The poem creates an image; describes an event, person, place, or thing; re-creates a moment in time.)
- Rhyme must help create meaning if it is to be used properly.
- Remember, a rhyming word group does not a poem make.

Work Together

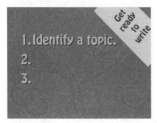

Slide 16

- Try writing one (or more) couplet as a group on a separate surface.
- Note: This is as easy as one, two, three.
- Start by choosing a topic.
- Get students thinking about possible topics. Ideas for topics might come from science class, social studies, or sports, or relate to a famous person, a character in a novel, or a place or point in history.

Slide 17

- Set up your separate surface, white board, or chart paper like this.
- Note that if your topic for this shared writing is, for instance, "monkeys," you would write that in the middle of the space.

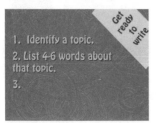

Slide 18

- Work together as a class to list four to six words about the chosen topic.

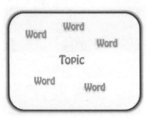

Slide 19

- Surround the topic with the descriptive words, as shown in the slide.

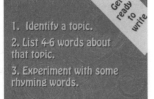

Slide 20

- Jot down some rhymes for the descriptive words.
- Note that we are not worried about context yet.

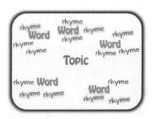

- Write one or two rhymes together as a class.
- Have students pair up to write another one on their own.
- Share a few aloud.
- Warning: It's going to be hard to hold students back at this point. They are going to be bursting with couplets.

Time to Write

Slide 22

- Have students gather their writing notebooks, pads, laptops, or scrap paper.
- Consider guiding your writers to a topic that's pertinent to your unit of study.
- Ask them to follow the pre-writing steps, one, two, three. (Display Slide 20 while they work.)
- Have students complete the pre-write and then ask them to begin composing their couplets.
- Notice that some (or many) students will want to just get busy writing the couplets and will want to skip the brainstorm.
- Explain that taking a few minutes to brainstorm will give them even more ideas.

Share

Slide 23: Time to Share

- Have some fun sharing couplets. They are short and can be real crowd pleasers. Note that couplets contain information and are not just rhyming word groups.
- Have students read their couplets aloud *at the same time*. A seat symphony!
- Have writers pop up and take turns reading theirs aloud.
- Emphasize that couplets may even be spontaneously combined to make a possibly combustible (and probably absurd) nonsense poem.
- Try a mash-up! If all students have written about a similar topic (a famous person, for instance), they may discover they can combine their texts to create a multifaceted poem.

Slide 24

- Couplets are succinct.
- Remember that couplets are a fun and memorable way to write about experiences.

Bonus Poems and Lesson Extensions

Slide 25

- These bonus poems have been selected to give you the opportunity to differentiate according to the needs of your classroom and to extend and reinforce the lesson.

Slide 26: "Rock Musician" by Jane Yolen

- Read the poem aloud, have a student read it, and/or play the audio.
- Enjoy!
- Introduce the poet (although with over 300 books to her name, she is probably familiar to students):
  - ○ Jane Yolen has been called the Hans Christian Andersen of America and the Aesop of the 20th century. She has won numerous awards for her poetry, picture books, and novels and is the recipient of six honorary doctorates in literature. It's hard to keep up with her, but you can find out more about her accomplishments and writing at www.janeyolen.com.

Slide 27: "The Star" by Jane Taylor

- This is probably one of the most famous of all couplet poems.
- Provide students with background information about the poem and the poet:
  - ○ Jane Taylor's poem was first published in 1806. She often wrote with her sister, Ann. The familiar tune to which this poem is most often sung is an English folk melody that existed before Jane and Ann were born. Jane was a bit of a daydreamer, as her siblings remembered her. She was home-schooled and died at the age of only 41.

Slide 28

- Many poets have written parodies of "The Star."
- Discuss how the parody on the slide follows the pattern of the original poem.
- Ask: Who is the poet speaking to in this parody? (The bat.)
- Click on the button to listen to and read the lyrics of the Muppets' parody. The Sesame Street parody video runs about 3 minutes.
- Note what Kermit and Don Music have to say about rhymes that just don't make sense.
- Ask: Does anybody have any ideas on how to write their own parody?
- If students are having difficulties stretching out their couplets, you might ask them to write some parodies of nursery rhymes.

Slide 29: "Martin Luther King" by Michael Salinger

- Read the poem aloud, have a student read it, and/or play the audio.

- Note that each couplet is not a complete sentence.

- Ask students to turn and talk: What is the effect of repeating the first line at the end of the poem? (When we circle back to the beginning, your audience will recognize you've reached the end of the poem.)

Slide 30: "Pout" by Sara Holbrook

- Explain that a couplet is a couplet no matter how the poet decides to place it on the page.

- Act this one out! Take pictures. It's a hoot.

ASSESSMENT

Here we provide a rubric you may choose to use. We provide this as a guide knowing that you may have other goals for your class. Don't feel compelled to assess every skill mentioned in this chart. We have had more success when we zero in on a skill or two with a lesson, but we want to afford you multiple options with these clinics.

Skill	3	2	1
Careful Reading	Demonstrates an understanding of couplets as distinguished from rhyming word groups.	Partially demonstrates an understanding of couplets as distinguished from rhyming word groups. May use a gratuitous rhyme along with some structured couplets.	Does not demonstrate an understanding of couplets as distinguished from rhyming word groups. Seems to use rhymes for rhyme's sake.
Structure and Organization	Demonstrates the ability to recognize and re-create a writing structure, such as a strong conclusion.	Partially demonstrates the ability to recognize and re-create a writing structure, such as a strong conclusion.	Does not demonstrate the ability to recognize and re-create a writing structure, such as a strong conclusion.
Conduct Short Research on a Subject	Demonstrates an understanding of the subject under investigation.	Partially demonstrates an understanding of the subject under investigation.	Does not demonstrate an understanding of the subject under investigation.
Speaking Skills	Consistently demonstrates effective presentation skills using good voice projection, inflection, pacing, eye contact, and stance.	Partially demonstrates effective presentation skills using good voice projection, inflection, pacing, eye contact, and stance.	Does not demonstrate effective presentation skills using good voice projection, inflection, pacing, eye contact, and stance.
Listening Skills	Actively participates in discussions about other students' work and is tuned in to student presentations.	Occasionally participates in discussions about other students' work and is tuned in to student presentations.	Does not participate in discussions about other students' work and is not tuned in to student presentations.

7

No Longer the Same

Building Comparisons

WHY TEACH THIS?

Things change. The phrase is not just a movie written by the unlikely duo of David Mamet and Shel Silverstein; it's a fact of life. *I used to be but now I am* is an adage to which we can all relate.

This writing clinic will help students build relevant comparisons into their writing. Understanding how to compare and contrast is a basic building-block skill that students need in order to be able to craft a strong argument, persuasive essay, or research paper. In this clinic, students will gain practice with this skill as they collect and use evidence and then produce writing—first through a personal connection and then with content area subject matter. Students will use multiple sources of research as they "build up" their pieces around a logical framework.

Michael: How's the old adage go—the only thing certain is change?

Sara: This clinic is loosely based on one of my favorite poetry writing exercises by fellow poet/educator Kenneth Koch. He was a pioneer in helping kids with their self-expression and in helping them chart change in themselves and understand their worlds through poetry.

CCSS AND CORRESPONDING ANCHOR STANDARDS

- **Demonstrate** command of the conventions of Standard English grammar and usage when writing or speaking.

  [4.L.1] [5.L.1] [6.L.1] [7.L.1] [8.L.1]

- **Analyze** the structure of texts, including how specific sentences, paragraphs, and larger portions of the text (e.g., a section, chapter, scene, or stanza) relate to each other and the whole.

  [4.RL.5] [5.RL.5] [6.RL.5] [7.RL.5] [8.RL.5]

- **Assess** how point of view or purpose shapes the content and style of a text.

  [4.RL.6] [5.RL.6] [6.RL.6] [7.RL.6] [8.RL.6]

- **Read** and comprehend complex literary and informational texts independently and proficiently.

  [4.RL.10] [5.RL.10] [6.RL.10] [7.RL.10] [8.RL.10]

- **Integrate** and evaluate information presented in diverse media and formats, including visually, quantitatively, and orally.

  [4.SL.2] [5.SL.2] [6.SL.2] [7.SL.2] [8.SL.2]

- **Write** informative/explanatory texts to examine and convey complex ideas and information clearly and accurately through the effective selection, organization, and analysis of content.

  [4.W.2] [5.W.2] [6.W.2] [7.W.2] [8.W.2]

- **Produce** clear and coherent writing in which the development, organization, and style are appropriate to task, purpose, and audience.

  [4.W.4] [5.W.4] [6.W.4] [7.W.4] [8.W.4]

- **Gather** relevant information from multiple print and digital sources, assess the credibility and accuracy of each source, and integrate the information while avoiding plagiarism.

  [4.W.8] [5.W.8] [6.W.8] [7.W.8] [8.W.8]

PRIOR TO THE LESSON

- Read through the entire lesson and review the slideshow to familiarize yourself with the clinic.

- Note that one of the bonus poems at the end of this clinic may be better suited to use as a model for your class than the one embedded in the clinic. Select the poem that works best for you and your students—your choice.

- Note that students will be making lists of details about how a topic has changed over time.

- Consider whether or not you would like students to write their comparison poems on a topic of classroom study. If so, have multiple research options available.

THE LESSON

Slide 1

- Introduce the teaching poets by name (Sara and Michael), as they will appear throughout this lesson.

Slide 2

- Read through the slide with students.

- Explain to students that we will follow a pattern to compare and contrast *what was* with *what is*.

- Let them know that we will use concrete details to support our comparisons.

- Explain that we are going to use this pattern to write about ourselves and/or our studies.

Slide 3

- Explain that this is a picture of a one-room schoolhouse (now a museum) in St. John's, North Dakota.

- Discuss for a moment what the students are seeing. (They may not recognize a potbellied stove or ink wells.)

- Have student turn and talk about things that have changed in schools since the 19th century.

- Ask: What do we still have?

- Ask: What do we no longer use?

- Ask: What is missing that we have now?

Slide 4

- Ask: besides schools, what other things have changed since the old days? (Transportation, communication, medicine, technology, etc.)

- Relate to students this story from Sara, or insert one of your own (please!).
  - "My grandfather was born in 1898. He used to say that when he was a boy, everyone had horses, but only really rich people had cars. By the time he was a man, everyone had cars and only rich people had horses."

- Ask: What are some changes that students have seen in their own worlds?

Slide 5

- Note: Not only do things such as schools, transportation, and communication change, we also change personally.

- Ask: What are some ways that we change personally?

- Ask: What is something that you used to like as a preschooler and now you've outgrown?

- Have students turn and talk for 2 minutes about memories of how they used to be.

Text Talk

Slide 6

- Read the poem aloud, have a student read it, and/or play the audio.
- Note that Michael is writing from the point of view of a student.
  - "In order to write this poem, I had to remember back and pretend I was a student. Although it was a (ahem) few years ago, I still remember."
- Ask students to turn and talk for 1 minute about the pattern of the poem.
- Ask: What do you notice about this pattern?
- Ask: How is the concluding line different? (It breaks the pattern.)

Time to Write

Slide 7

- Have students get out paper, notebooks, pads, or computers.
- Note that this clinic is a little different because of its personal nature.
- Tell students that instead of writing together first, we will write individually using Michael's poem as a model.
- Explain that later we will compose a content area piece as a group.

Slide 8

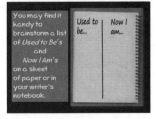

- Instruct the students to first brainstorm a written list of personal *Used to be's* and *Now I am's*. (Three or four of each will get them started.)
  - Remind them that they already have done a lot of this brainstorming through their earlier conversations.
  - Explain that we can of course substitute other verbs for *be* and *am*, such as *I used to climb on my mom's lap, now I climb mountains* or *I used to crawl, now I can skateboard*. See the example on the next slide.

Slide 9

- Note that this is the sequence pattern that we are going to use to draft our poem.
- Ask students to choose three or four examples of things from their brainstorm that have changed about them.
- Remind students to substitute other verbs (as shown on the previous slide), such as "I used to climb on my mom's lap, now I climb mountains." Or, "I used to crawl, now I can skateboard." Invite them to offer other suggestions.
- Point out the images on the slide and ask students to call out some other action verbs they might use.
- Reinforce that we are looking for concrete details—evidence to support the comparisons and prove that they have changed.

- Explain that saying "I used to be cute and now I am ugly" is not good enough. (See Clinic 1, Objective Versus Subjective.) Those are just opinion words, and writers will want to cite specific examples.

- Ask each student to conclude their Version 1 with a true statement about themselves, perhaps with something they like or do not like, breaking the pattern, and ending the poem.

- Note: This is a writing exercise that we have adapted from the famous educational poet Kenneth Koch. If you or your students want more information about him, please check out his book *Wishes, Lies, and Dreams*, an oldie but goodie.

Share

Slide 10

- Ask students to share their poems with a partner or in a small group.

- Explain to students that they have an important role as a listener.

- Make students aware that they should listen to see if their sharing partner has followed the pattern and used specific examples rather than opinions.

- Tell partners that they should be ready with helpful suggestions for improvement.

- Provide students with this hint: "I used to be fast, now I am faster" is not specific enough.

- Invite a couple of students to share with the class after they have shared with their partners.

Time to Revise (Expand)

Slide 11

- Ask students to revisit Michael's Version 1.

- Explain: Often when we are revising, we are looking for places to cut unnecessary words.

- Explain that this time, we want to expand what we wrote.

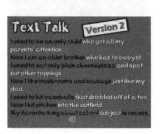

Slide 12

- Read through the revisions in white that Michael made to his Version 1.

- Ask: What might be another idea that Michael could have used to expand his first line? (For instance, "I used to be an only child who had no one to play with" or "I didn't have to share my toys.")

- Ask students to revisit their Version 1s and add a new idea to each line.

- Note that Michael also took out some words in the last line and chose a more specific word.

- Note that we are expanding our Version 1 with specific examples, not just adding words but citing evidence to support our ideas.

Slide 13: Part 2: Changing Your Point of View

- Explain to students that in the second part of this exercise, we will write from another's point of view.

- Let students know that in order to discover this point of view, we will most likely have to do research.

Text Talk

Slide 14: "American Bison" by Sara Holbrook

- Read the poem aloud, have a student read it, and/or play the audio.

- Note: This poem is written from the point of view of the bison.

- Ask: What is the same about this piece and the piece that you just wrote? (Structure.)

- Ask: What is different about this piece compared to the pieces that you just wrote? (It is written from a different point of view.)

- Let students know what Sara had to say about the poem:
  - "I researched simple facts about the American bison to draft this Version 1 by just using one source: Wikipedia."
  - "This single source gave me enough information to complete a first draft."

Slide 15

- Read through Version 2 of "American Bison."

- Let students know what Sara had to say about the poem:
  - "I used multiple sources for research to gather details to further develop my piece on the bison. These included the Smithsonian Zoo, greatamericanbison.com, and other sites."
  - "Researching the bison just made me think of more questions."

- Ask students to turn and talk for 1 minute: If you were to continue to develop this piece of writing, what questions would you want to research? What more do you want to know about the bison?

Time to Write

Slide 16

- Take this opportunity to steer students to your current unit of study.

- Have students turn and talk about potential topics.

- Consider having students write in pairs or on their own.

Slide 17

- As you walk them through the writing process, remind them that it may be sufficient to use one research source for Version 1.

- Explain that they will want to consult a variety of research sources in order to verify and/or expand facts used in their Version 2.

- Use Michael's poem or the poem about the American bison for student writing models.
- Alternately, you may want to craft one on the board as a group.

Slide 18

- Tell students that the phrase "I used to be, but now I am" is useful for them to use as a framework to compare what was to what is.
- Explain to students that second drafts offer opportunities to add key details.

Bonus Poems and Lesson Extensions

Slide 19

- These bonus poems have been selected to give you the opportunity to differentiate according to the needs of your classroom and to extend and reinforce the lesson.

Slide 20: "I Used to Be" by Elizabeth Thomas

- Read the poem aloud, have a student read it, and/or play the audio (on the next slide).
- Ask students to listen for the original structure as the poem is read. (I used to be, but now I am.)
- Ask: How does Elizabeth use specific images to stretch her ideas? (The poem is rich with visual language.)

Slide 21

- Ask students if the poet is using similes or metaphors to build her comparison. (Metaphors.)
- Provide students with some background on the poet:
  - Elizabeth Thomas is a teaching poet who divides her time between homes in Connecticut and Florida. Elizabeth is widely published and is a coach of the CT Brave New Voices Teen Poetry Slam team. You can read more about her at www.upwordspoetry.com/EBio.htm.

Slide 22: "Transience" by Sara Holbrook

- Read the poem aloud, have a student read it, and/or play the audio.
- Ask: Why do you think the poets chose this poem to go along with the writing exercise we just did? (It is about change.)
- Ask: What does Sara mean by the line "Today is tomorrow's laundry, guaranteed to shrink with every wash"? (Memories fade and shrink with time.)
- Ask students to offer observations of change in their lives and their worlds.

ASSESSMENT

Here we provide a rubric you may choose to use. We provide this as a guide knowing that you may have other goals for your class. Don't feel compelled to assess every skill mentioned in this chart. We have had more success when we zero in on a skill or two with a lesson, but we want to afford you multiple options with these clinics.

Skill	3	2	1
Careful Reading	Demonstrates, through classroom discussion and writing, an understanding of the impact of word choice on meaning and tone.	Partially demonstrates, through classroom discussion and writing, an understanding of the impact of word choice on meaning and tone.	Does not demonstrate, through classroom discussion and writing, an understanding of the impact of word choice on meaning and tone.
Structure and Organization	Demonstrates the ability to recognize and re-create a writing structure, such as a strong conclusion.	Partially demonstrates the ability to recognize and re-create a writing structure, such as a strong conclusion.	Does not demonstrate the ability to recognize and re-create a writing structure, such as a strong conclusion.
Grammar Conventions	Demonstrates an understanding of present and past tenses and uses them logically. Maintains subject-verb agreement.	Partially demonstrates an understanding of past and present tenses. May confuse subject-verb agreement occasionally.	Does not demonstrate an understanding of present and past tenses. Does not maintain subject-verb agreement.
Information Gathering	Demonstrates the ability to gather relevant information from multiple print and digital sources, assess the credibility and accuracy of each source, and integrate the information while avoiding plagiarism.	Partially demonstrates the ability to gather relevant information. May not incorporate multiple sources, or some "facts" may not be correct.	Does not demonstrate an understanding of how to gather relevant research. Uses no research materials or simply cuts and pastes information.
Speaking Skills	Consistently demonstrates effective presentation skills using good voice projection, inflection, pacing, eye contact, and stance.	Partially demonstrates effective presentation skills using good voice projection, inflection, pacing, eye contact, and stance.	Does not demonstrate effective presentation skills using good voice projection, inflection, pacing, eye contact, and stance.
Listening Skills	Actively participates in discussions about other students' work and is tuned in to student presentations.	Occasionally participates in discussions about other students' work and is tuned in to student presentations.	Does not participate in discussions about other students' work and is not tuned in to student presentations.

8

The Questioning Poem

A Way of Wondering

WHY TEACH THIS?

How do lizards walk on water?

What makes a tornado spin?

Why did the Protestants and the Catholics in Ireland fight?

Remember the last question that sent you to the Internet to find an answer? Remember the sense of urgency? How you typed in your question and began to prioritize the answers? Were you looking for text or an image? Did one lead you to the other? When you found your answer, did that lead you to more questions?

In order to encourage our students to become independent thinkers and life-long learners, we must first foster curiosity in every content area and discipline. At every grade level. In every classroom. Daily and diligently. Then we must equip them with the skills they need to find answers to those questions. As they mature and go on to attend college and/or enter the workplace, they will be expected to ask relevant questions. When they go on to become critical consumers and productive world citizens, they will come to understand that effective and applicable questions lie at the heart of all pertinent research.

In this clinic, students will read and analyze a poem that simply asks questions of the reader. They will then work as a group to produce a model poem composed of questions; they will collaborate in small groups to research and write a questioning poem. Finally, they will share their poems aloud, actively listening and speaking. The questions they raise will inspire them to dig deeper into relevant content areas—through the use of fiction and nonfiction—to ask more questions and find answers.

You may also use this clinic as a source of data about teaching and learning as you begin exploring a new content area unit or a piece of historical fiction. You may find other uses for assigning a questioning poem (we hope you will!) as this activity does the following:

- Actively involves students in their own learning
- Helps you clarify your goals for a given unit
- Helps you assess students' prior knowledge of an upcoming unit of study

Knowing what your students know and don't know, what they wonder about, and what their glaring misperceptions are will help make your instruction more purposeful.

Sara: We don't have to have all the answers to write a poem. I write about what I know but also what I wonder about.

Michael: Another way to look at the *what I know* and *what I wonder* template is as an assessment of prior knowledge—something that really helps going into a new unit.

CCSS AND CORRESPONDING ANCHOR STANDARDS

- **Prepare** for and participate effectively in a range of conversations and collaborations with diverse partners, building on others' ideas and expressing their own clearly and persuasively.

  [4.SL.1] [5.SL.1] [6.SL.1] [7.SL.1] [8.SL.1]

- **Integrate** and evaluate information presented in diverse media and formats, including visually, quantitatively, and orally.

  [4.SL.2] [5.SL.2] [6.SL.2] [7.SL.2] [8.SL.2]

- **Produce** clear and coherent writing in which the development, organization, and style are appropriate to task, purpose, and audience.

  [4.W.4] [5.W.4] [6.W.4] [7.W.4] [8.W.4]

- **Gather** relevant information from multiple print and digital sources, assess the credibility and accuracy of each source, and integrate the information while avoiding plagiarism.

  [4.W.8] [5.W.8] [6.W.8] [7.W.8] [8.W.8]

PRIOR TO THE LESSON

- Read through the entire lesson and review the slideshow to familiarize yourself with the clinic.
- Consider substituting a current topic of study for the one provided (a lizard) if you think it will further your classroom goals.

- Note that one of the bonus poems at the end of this clinic may be better suited to use as a model for your class than the one embedded in the clinic. Select the poem that works best for you and your students—your choice.

- Note that students will need their writing notebooks, index cards, or loose-leaf paper.

THE LESSON

Slide 1

- Introduce the teaching poets by name (Sara and Michael), as they will appear throughout this lesson.

Slide 2

- Explain to students that they are going to look at a subject new to them and gather questions about it.

- Let students know that they are then going to collaborate to compose a poem from those questions.

- Tell students that they are going to experience how asking questions *before* they delve into a subject can lead to deeper thinking.

Slide 3

- Tell students that as writers, they will often be told to write what they know.

Slide 4

- Explain to students that it's also okay for them to write about things that they wonder about.

Text Talk

Slide 5: "What's the Point?" by Sara Holbrook

- Read the poem aloud, have a student read it, and/or play the audio.

- Note that this is a model of a questioning poem. It doesn't attempt to answer the questions; it just poses them.

- Ask: Does the poet have a point in this poem, even though she doesn't answer any of the questions? (Entertain suggestions, no right or wrong answer.)

- Ask: Can you identify any part of this poem that is not a question? What purpose does that serve in the poem? (It gives a little background context to the questions.)

Work Together

Slide 6

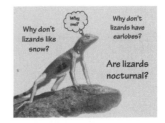

- Announce to students that they are going to compose a model questioning poem about a lizard.
- Consider whether or not you would like to choose another topic for your model poem (something that is related to your upcoming unit).
- Read through the model questions about the lizard that appear on the slide.
- Have students turn and talk in pairs or small groups and instruct them to jot down at least three questions they have about lizards (or your selected topic).

Slide 7

- Have each group of students look at their questions and identify one or two of them that are the most important.
- Have each group of students send a representative to write a question or two on the board.
- Lead the class in a discussion of these questions.
- Ask: Do you see any duplicates?
- Ask: Do these questions lead you to any other questions?
- Take suggestions and write down additional questions.
- Explain that you will now use these questions to write a poem together.
- Ask: Which question should we choose to start our poem?
- Write the poem on the board or chart paper as you continue to ask, "What's next?"
- Ask: Do we want to add any lines or words that are not questions? (Look back to Slide 5 to see how the poet inserted background information.)
- Keep in mind that there is no need to spend too much time on this. As soon as you think students have an understanding of the process, it will be time for them to write on their own in small groups.

Time to Write

Slide 8

- Ask students to form small groups of three or four.
- Distribute note cards or small pieces of recycled paper.

- Explain that they are beginning a unit on _____. (Insert subject matter: hurricanes, oceans, energy, the renaissance, industrial revolution, a novel, whatever.)
- Let students know that they should have their notebooks handy.

Slide 9

- Inform students that while they are working in their small groups, they should be following the same steps that they did in the large group.
- Give students 3–5 minutes to write their questions.
- Provide students with an image or research materials, as needed.
- Ask students to pool their questions in their small groups, spread them out on a flat surface, and examine what they have.
- Ask them to eliminate the duplicates.
- Ask them to select one student in the group to be the scribe.
- Reinforce that this person is not doing all the work, but rather transcribing the collaborative ideas of the group.
- Have students collaborate to write their questioning poem.
- Ask: Do you want to add any lines or words that are not questions? (Look back to Slide 5 to see how the poet inserted background information or refer to the model poem that the class wrote together.)
- Once the poem is composed, ask everyone in the group to make a copy in his or her own notebook, pad, or computer.

Share

Slide 10

- Announce that the groups will be presenting their poems to the rest of the class.
- Ask the groups to make sure everyone has a part in the presentation.
- Encourage students to have some fun with this. Suggest that they are free to make background rhythms and sound effects and to stage the poem to fit the material and the audience.
- Provide feedback and positive reinforcement to students after each presentation. Let students know that you are hearing some good questions, and highlight those questions that you think are among the best. Keep in mind that it's ideal to have students post their questioning poems in the classroom and/or on a classroom blog.

Slide 11

- Have students turn and talk about what they will remember from this lesson.
- Consider posting the questioning poems in the classroom so that you can easily reference them as you proceed through your unit.

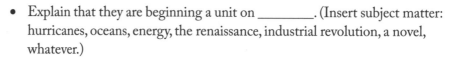

- Refer back to the poems periodically and say something like "Remember? That is one of the questions you had before we started the unit."

Bonus Poems and Lesson Extensions

Slide 12

- These bonus poems have been selected to give you the opportunity to differentiate according to the needs of your classroom and to extend and reinforce the lesson.

Slide 13: "A Question" by Robert Frost

- Click on the button on the slide to go to the poem, or you can find it here: http://en.wikipedia.org/wiki/A_Question_(poem).

- Read the poem aloud or have a student read the poem. The poem is short (four lines), so reread as needed for deeper understanding.

- Ask: Does anyone in the class have a scar from a cut or surgery? (That's a body scar.)

- Ask: What does the poet mean by a soul scar? What could cause such a scar? (Death of a loved one, disappointment, a putdown.)

- Ask students to turn and talk about the meaning of the poem.

- Ask: What is the big question Frost is asking? (No right or wrong answers here; entertain suggestions.)

- Note: Frost does not give us a simple answer.

- Provide students with the following background information about the poem:
  - "A Question" is a poem by American poet Robert Frost, first published in 1942 in *A Witness Tree*. For more information about Robert Frost, visit www.poets.org/poet.php/prmPID/192.

Slide 14: "Marvelous Math" by Rebecca Kai Dotlich

- Ask: Ever wonder what you are doing in school?

- Ask: Who invented math class? Why do you need to know about math?

- Ask: How does the poet make an argument for understanding math by just asking questions? (She asks questions about the world that only mathematics can help her answer.)

- Provide students with some background information about the poet:
  - Rebecca Kai Dotlich writes poetry and picture books. From *Lemonade Sun* to *Rumbling Riddles*, you can find out more about Rebecca, her books, and her school visits by going to www.rebeccakaidotlich.com.

Slide 15: "Kind" by Sara Holbrook

- Read the poem aloud, have a student read it, and/or play the audio.
- Point out that Sara asks a lot of questions here.
- Ask: What's the big question she is asking here?
- Ask students to turn and talk.
- Discuss.

Slide 16: "Where Does the Sky Begin?" by Michael Salinger

- Read the poem aloud, have a student read it, and/or play the audio.
- Ask: What are all these questions about?
- Ask: Where might we go to research answers to these questions?
- Ask: If you were the author of this poem, what would you want to know about the sky and the atmosphere?

ASSESSMENT

Here we provide a rubric you may choose to use. We provide this as a guide knowing that you may have other goals for your class. Don't feel compelled to assess every skill mentioned in this chart. We have had more success when we zero in on a skill or two with a lesson, but we want to afford you multiple options with these clinics.

Skill	3	2	1
Careful Reading	Demonstrates, through classroom discussion and writing, an understanding of the impact of word choice on meaning and tone.	Partially demonstrates, through classroom discussion and writing, an understanding of the impact of word choice on meaning and tone.	Does not demonstrate, through classroom discussion and writing, an understanding of the impact of word choice on meaning and tone.
Structure and Organization	Demonstrates the ability to recognize and re-create a writing structure composed of questions appropriate to the classroom task at hand.	Partially demonstrates the ability to recognize and re-create a writing structure composed of questions. May include duplicate questions or questions that are not pertinent.	Does not demonstrate the ability to recognize and re-create a writing structure that is composed of questions. Composes piece using statements or irrelevant questions.
Writing Collaboratively	Demonstrates the ability to engage in collaborative civil discourse and discussion that results in a piece of writing with shared authorship.	Shows some evidence of collaboration, but discussion and output are obviously not a group effort.	Group is unable to collaborate. Work produced is obviously created by one author or is unfinished.
Speaking Skills	Consistently demonstrates effective presentation skills using good voice projection, inflection, pacing, eye contact, and stance.	Partially demonstrates effective presentation skills using good voice projection, inflection, pacing, eye contact, and stance.	Does not demonstrate effective presentation skills using good voice projection, inflection, pacing, eye contact, and stance.
Listening Skills	Actively participates in discussions about other students' work and is tuned in to student presentations.	Occasionally participates in discussions about other students' work and is tuned in to student presentations.	Does not participate in discussions about other students' work and is not tuned in to student presentations.

Refrain

Come Again?

WHY TEACH THIS?

This writing clinic will help students understand the power of a refrain. Repetition is one of the elements of persuasive as well as creative writing.

Repetition is an essential tool in any writer's box. As writers and teachers we innately know this, but research backs up this hypothesis. Studies by leading social psychologists J. T. Cacioppo and Richard Petty have shown that low to moderate levels of repetition in a message tend to create greater agreement with the message, in addition to producing greater recall.

Repetition is an essential tool in any writer's box. Of course, too much repetition gets monotonous and actually starts to cause our readers to tune out from the message. This clinic will help students identify words and phrases worth repeating in their writing.

Michael: You can say that again.

Sara: Let's just do the clinic.

Reference

Cacioppo, J. T., & Petty, R. E. (1979). Effects of Message Repetition and Position on Cognitive Response, Recall, and Persuasion. *Journal of Personality and Social Psychology, 37,* 97–109.

CCSS AND CORRESPONDING ANCHOR STANDARDS

- **Demonstrate** understanding of word relationships and nuances in word meanings.

  [4.L.5] [5.L.5] [6.L.5] [7.L.5] [8.L.5]

- **Determine** central ideas or themes of a text and analyze their development; summarize the key supporting details and ideas.

  [4.RIT.2] [5.RIT.2] [6.RIT.2] [7.RIT.2] [8.RIT.2]

- **Read** and comprehend complex literary and informational texts independently.

  [4.RL.10] [5.RL.10] [6.RL.10] [7.RL.10] [8.RL.10]

- **Write** informative/explanatory texts to examine and convey complex ideas and information clearly and accurately through the effective selection, organization, and analysis of content.

  [4.W.2] [5.W.2] [6.W.2] [7.W.2] [8.W.2]

- **Produce** clear and coherent writing in which the development, organization, and style are appropriate to task, purpose, and audience.

  [4.W.4] [5.W.4] [6.W.4] [7.W.4] [8.W.4]

PRIOR TO THE LESSON

- Read through the entire lesson and review the slideshow to familiarize yourself with the clinic.

- Depending on the length of your class, this lesson may take two periods.

- Check out the bonus poems at the end of this clinic. You may find one better suited to your class than the one embedded in the clinic. Feel free to move slides around to fit your classroom needs.

- Set up a separate surface (chart paper or white board) on which to compose a poem written collectively by you and your students.

- Couplets are used and referred to in this lesson. You may want to refer back to the lesson on couplets (Clinic 6).

THE LESSON

Slide 1

- Introduce the teaching poets by name (Sara and Michael), as they will appear throughout this lesson.

Slide 2

- Read this slide aloud, or have a student read it.

- Explain that we are going to examine the use of refrain in writing and we are going to write using a refrain.

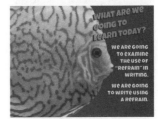

Slide 3

- Refrains might be included in poems, speeches, persuasive editorials, and commercials.

- Ask: Can you think of a song that has a refrain? (From "Old MacDonald" to Mozart to Lady Gaga, many musicians use refrains.)

Slide 4

- Use this pattern as the basis for writing in this lesson:
  - Stanza-refrain, stanza-refrain, stanza-refrain.

Slide 5

- This is the lead-in question for our sample refrain poem.
- Ask: Ever been in trouble for something that was not your fault?

Text Talk

Slide 6

- This is the refrain line (based on our lead-in question) that students will repeat as you read through the poem.
- Have them say it aloud.

Slides 7–11

- Read the words in yellow.
- Have students read the refrain line.

Slide 12

- Examine the entire poem and discuss how it is constructed.
- Point out that in this poem there are stanzas that appear between the refrains. In this case, the stanzas that separate the refrains are made of up of rhyming couplets.
- Note how the pattern changes at the end of the poem.
- Emphasize to your students that breaking a pattern is a powerful writing strategy.

Work Together

Slide 13

- Prepare a separate surface (white board, chart paper) on which you will compose a poem with your students.

Slide 14

- Here we are writing about the word *adrenaline*.

- Invite students to consult a reference source (dictionary, thesaurus, Wikipedia) to help them identify two important words about adrenaline.

- Don't dig in too deeply just yet—the students will have that opportunity later, when they compose the stanzas.

Slide 15

- Choose one of the important words to become the refrain.

- Here we chose the word *energy*.

- Place that word three times on your writing surface with space in between the lines.

Slide 16

- Add the second important word at the bottom, as it will become the concluding line.

Slide 17

- The spaces you left between the refrain words are where you will write your supporting text.

- Invite students to consult additional research sources to come up with the details needed for these intervening lines.

- Take suggestions from the class as they come up with them.

- Remind students that we are not concerning ourselves with rhyme at this time.

- Read the completed poems aloud together a couple of times. Divide up the stanzas and refrains, and have different sections of the class take different parts.

Time to Write

Slide 18

- Have students take out their notebooks, pads, or laptops.

- Give students the option of writing on their own or in pairs.

Slide 19

- Leave this slide showing as you walk the students through their writing process.

- Steer students to your current unit of study if you wish.

- Invite students to write about a word, a person, an event, a math or science concept, a place, a sport. Really, anything!
- Suggest that if students use rhyming couplets as stanzas, they may wish to make edits for rhythm and content.

Share

Slide 20

- Have students share their poems (if they haven't already) with a partner or with their table groups.
- Ask a few students to share with the class.

Slide 21

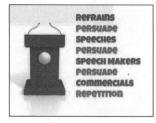

- Poetry and music aren't the only places where we see refrains.
- Persuasive speeches and commercials also use refrains.
- Ask: Why do you think people use refrains when they are trying to persuade? (Because they want their audience to remember an idea or product.)
- Ask: Do you think using a repeated refrain in persuasion works? (Yes, as long as the repetition doesn't become monotonous.)

Slide 22: Four Speeches Utilizing Refrain

- 1. President Obama used a refrain 17 times in his speech to Congress on September 8, 2011.
    - Click on the hyperlink to hear a 2:12-minute clip showing the use of refrain.
    - Find the full text of the speech online if you want to compare the written to the spoken word.
- 2. Ronald Reagan used refrain in a speech delivered on October 28, 1980, right before the presidential election.
    - Click on the hyperlink to hear the clip. It is only a little over a minute long.
- 3. Hillary Clinton (then First Lady) used refrain in a speech delivered in September 1995 to the United Nations 4th World Plenary Session on Women in Beijing, China.
    - Click on the hyperlink to hear the speech and see the text.
    - Note: This is a long speech. She begins using the refrain line 12:15 minutes into the speech.
- 4. Martin Luther King Jr. used refrain in his "I Have a Dream" speech.
    - Click on the hyperlink to hear a beautifully executed clip, highlighting the refrain. (Many others are available online.)
    - Ask: What is he trying to persuade the American public to do?
- Consider using these sample speeches as a springboard for students to write their own persuasive speeches using a repeated phrase.

Slide 23

- Ask: What are some uses of refrain in writing?

Bonus Poems and Lesson Extensions

Slide 24

- These bonus poems have been selected to give you the opportunity to differentiate according to the needs of your classroom and to extend and reinforce the lesson.

Slide 25: "The Farewell of a Virginia Slave Mother to Her Daughters Sold Into Southern Bondage" by John Greenleaf Whittier

- Note: This is a poem and not a political speech as we know them today. However, the poem is political in its theme.

- Read through this poem and ask students to read the yellow refrain line as you read the intervening text and/or play the audio.

- Pause after the first read-through and ask if the meanings of any of the words are unclear.

- Ask: Was Whittier attempting to persuade his audience? (Yes, he was informing the public about the realities of slave sales. He was trying to change the minds of those in the audience.)

- Ask: What is the evidence that Whittier presented to help in his persuasion? (He details how a child may be sold and never be seen by her mother again.)

- Ask: What is the effect of the use of a refrain? (It holds the poem together and brings his audience along, reinforcing the story.)

- Pictured here are only the first verses of this poem. The complete text of the poem can be found at www.bartleby.com/248/213.html.

- Provide students with some background information about the poet:

  o John Greenleaf Whittier wrote this poem in 1838. He was from Massachusetts, a Quaker who devoted his life and talents to the abolitionist movement for more than 20 years. He was a performance poet, renting halls to give poetry readings and reading on street corners trying to direct the attention of the public to the abolitionist movement. For more information about Whittier visit www.johngreenleafwhittier.com.

Slide 26: "The Feisty Pig of France" by David Harrison

- Read the poem aloud (two slides), have a couple of students read it, and/or play the audio.

- Explain that this poem is a villanelle. For more information about this poetry form, check online sources such as http://en.wikipedia.org/wiki/Villanelle.

Slide 27

- A villanelle is a much more complex form than a simple refrain.
- Explain that villanelles are built on repeating lines.
- Ask students to root around in this poem to find the pattern.
- Provide students with some background information about the author:
  - David Harrison is the author of more than 80 books for kids and adults. For more information about David and his lively books, please visit www.davidlharrison.com. While you are there, be sure to click on the link to his blog, which is full of classroom ideas and poetry.

Slide 28: "Dog Daze" by Sara Holbrook

- Read the black words and ask students to read the red refrain lines.
- Explain that the dog in this picture is Sara and Michael's dog Lili.
- Ask: What is Lili saying in this refrain poem? (She wants to run away from home.)
- Ask: Have you ever felt like Lili?

ASSESSMENT

Here we provide a rubric you may choose to use. We provide this as a guide knowing that you may have other goals for your class. Don't feel compelled to assess every skill mentioned in this chart. We have had more success when we zero in on a skill or two with a lesson, but we want to afford you multiple options with these clinics.

Skill	3	2	1
Careful Reading	Demonstrates an understanding of the impact of specific word choice and the relationship between the refrain and the intervening lines.	Partially demonstrates an understanding of the impact of specific word choice, but may have a weak conclusion or perhaps may not have chosen the most appropriate words for the refrain.	Does not demonstrate an understanding of the impact of a specific word choice when choosing a refrain. May not follow an established pattern, and intervening lines may not be relevant.
Structure and Organization	Demonstrates the ability to recognize and replicate a writing structure. Includes an apt refrain and a strong conclusion.	Partially demonstrates the ability to recognize and replicate a writing structure, but may misstep by forgetting or inadvertently repeating an intervening line.	Does not demonstrate the ability to recognize and replicate a writing structure. The piece has no refrain or intervening lines.
Connotative Word Meaning	Demonstrates an understanding of connotative word meanings when selecting words for the refrain and the conclusion. Crafts relevant intervening lines.	Occasionally demonstrates an understanding of connotative word meanings. May have a conclusion or an intervening line that is weak.	Does not demonstrate an understanding of connotative word meanings. The choice of refrain and/or intervening lines shows no evidence of thoughtful word choice.
Speaking Skills	Consistently demonstrates effective presentation skills using good voice projection, inflection, pacing, eye contact, and stance.	Partially demonstrates effective presentation skills using good voice projection, inflection, pacing, eye contact, and stance.	Does not demonstrate effective presentation skills using good voice projection, inflection, pacing, eye contact, and stance.
Listening Skills	Actively participates in discussing other students' work and is tuned in to student presentations.	Occasionally participates in discussing other students' work and is tuned in to student presentations.	Does not participate in discussing other students' work and is not tuned in to student presentations.

10

Personification

A Word Walks in . . .

WHY TEACH THIS?

Personification is possibly the most ubiquitous form of figurative language. Words and phrases that animate our descriptions of objects and feelings with human traits help our readers and listeners manufacture a picture of what we are trying to communicate. Time can fly, it can drag, tick by, or it might even run out. That neon sign might be screaming for attention while a bucolic log cabin hides among the pines.

This lesson is designed to encourage students to attach physical characteristics to otherwise intangible emotional states by collecting and citing evidence rather than subjective synonyms. We demonstrate *show, don't tell* by asking students to use objective evidence to tell us *how* (*show* minus the *s*) a particular emotion acts within a well-structured sequence.

Demonstrating an understanding of figurative language is a key Common Core State Standard, and by employing well-grounded personification in their own writing, students will better be able to identify and understand its use in the text they read.

Sara: Personification makes words cartwheel and skip.

Michael: Hopefully the language doesn't trip over itself.

CCSS AND CORRESPONDING ANCHOR STANDARDS

- **Read** closely to determine what the text says explicitly and to make logical inferences from it; cite specific textual evidence when writing or speaking to support conclusions drawn from the text.

  [4.RL.1] [5.RL.1] [6.RL.1] [7.RL.1] [8.RL.1]

- **Interpret** words and phrases as they are used in a text, including determining technical, connotative, and figurative meanings, and analyze how specific word choices shape meaning or tone.

  [4.RL.4] [5.RL.4] [6.RL.4] [7.RL.4] [8.RL.4]

- **Demonstrate** understanding of figurative language, word relationships, and nuances in word meanings.

  [4.L.5] [5.L.5] [6.L.5] [7.L.5] [8.L.5]

- **Read** and comprehend complex literary and informational texts independently and proficiently.

  [4.RL.10] [5.RL.10] [6.RL.10] [7.RL.10] [8.RL.10]

- **Interpret** words and phrases as they are used in a text, including determining technical, connotative, and figurative meanings, and analyze how specific word choices shape meaning or tone.

  [4.RIT.4] [5.RIT.4] [6.RIT.4] [7.RIT.4] [8.RIT.4]

- **Write** informative/explanatory texts to examine a topic, convey ideas, concepts, and information through the selection, organization, and analysis of relevant content.

  [4.W.2] [5.W.2] [6.W.2] [7.W.2] [8.W.2]

- **Write** narrative to develop real or imagined experiences or events using effective technique, well-chosen details, and well-structured sequences.

  [4.W.3] [5.W.3] [6.W.3] [7.W.3] [8.W.3]

- **Produce** clear and coherent writing in which the development, organization, and style are appropriate to task, purpose, and audience.

  [4.W.4] [5.W.4] [6.W.4] [7.W.4] [8.W.4]

PRIOR TO THE LESSON

- Read through the entire lesson and review the slideshow to familiarize yourself with the clinic.

- Set up a separate surface (chart paper or white board) on which to compose a poem written collectively by you and your students.

- Note that one of the bonus poems at the end of this clinic may be better suited to use as a model for your class than the one embedded in the clinic. Select the poem that works best for you and your students— your choice.

THE LESSON

Slide 1

- Introduce the teaching poets by name (Sara and Michael), as they will appear throughout this clinic.

Slide 2

- Read through the lesson goals with students and add any additional goals you may have for this lesson.

- Explain that students will be learning about a fun method that they can use to describe an event or a feeling using physical evidence.

- Tell students that they will be learning about how to compose a poem using personification.

- Reveal to students that you will be putting motion into words.

Slide 3

- Tell students that the headline running down the side of this slide may be hard to read, but that the young man's body language is not.

- Have students turn and talk for a minute about what words they might use to describe this guy.

- Invite students to offer their ideas to the class. (Responses might include words such as *tired, discouraged, withdrawn.*)

- Ask: What is the evidence that led you to this conclusion? (Head in hands, bowed head.)

- Ask: Could we say that this student "personifies" one of these words? (Yes!)

- Give students an example of how this works by putting one of their observations into a sentence. "Discouraged hid his head in his hands."

Text Talk

Slide 4: "Jubilant" by Michael Salinger

- Read the poem aloud, have a student read it, and/or play the audio.

- Point out that in this poem, Michael describes Jubilant as being in a "very, very, good mood."

- Ask: What physical evidence does he cite to support his statement?

Work Together

Slide 5

- Announce: We are going to play a game called Pass the Movement.

- Ask students to stand beside their desks and push in their chairs.

- Begin by loosening everyone up. Have students put their hands in the air, make jazz hands, put their hands on their hips, and so on. These are just a few simple motions to get students' hands out of their pockets.

- Explain how Pass the Movement works: You will make a motion and everyone in the class will copy your actions.

- Turn to the student next to you and say, "Pass." (We often start by clenching fists and marching in place, looking determined.)

- Indicate that everyone should copy what that student is doing.

- Turn to the person beside you and indicate that she should do a different movement, and that everyone should copy her.

- Continue around the room until everyone has a chance.

- Note: We always outlaw touching others or throwing ourselves on the floor.

Slide 6

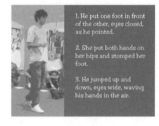

- Choose three enthusiastic volunteers to come to the front of the class.

- Have everyone else return to their seats.

- Ask each of these three students to re-create their motions, one at a time.

- On a separate surface, write down one sentence to describe each of the students' actions (three sentences total). Have each sentence begin with the pronoun *He* or *She*.

- Provide this sample of a descriptive sentence: *He put one foot in front of the other, eyes closed, as he pointed.*

Slide 7

- You will have three descriptive sentences that read something like this:
  - *He put one foot in front of the other, eyes closed, as he pointed.*
  - *She put both hands on her hips and stomped her foot.*
  - *He jumped up and down, eyes wide, waving his hands in the air.*

- Instruct your enthusiastic volunteers to return to their seats.

- Point out that what we now have are three images, and that these images serve as descriptive evidence that can be dropped into an essay, a poem, a story, or a science report.

Slide 8

- Choose one of the image descriptions.

- Ask: If a writer used this to describe a character in a story, what might that character be feeling?

- Have students turn and talk for 30 seconds to come up with some ideas.

- Note that some possible ideas may include the words *angry, frustrated, miffed,* or *stubborn.*

- Choose one of these words and rewrite the sentence.

Slide 9

- Rewrite the sentence substituting the emotion for the pronoun.

- Ask: What did we just do? (We personified the word *stubborn.*)

Slide 10

- Brainstorm some more feelings and create an emotional word wall.
- Get started with these; let the class come up with more.
- Limit your brainstorm to 1.5 or 2 minutes.
- Indicate that you are going to choose one of these words and write a model poem.
- Vote to select a word.
- Reassure students that they will have an opportunity to write their own poems and that they shouldn't be disappointed if their favorite feeling was not chosen.

Slide 11

- Write the selected feeling at the top of the page, as pictured in this slide.
- Here we have selected *stubborn*. Chances are you have chosen a different word. The clinic steps will remain the same.
- Remind students that one of our challenges as writers, whether we are writing a story, a poem, or a science report, is determining how to put action into words.
- Begin Version 1 with a sentence describing an action. Ask everyone to try on the feeling—to pretend they are feeling *stubborn* (or to pretend they are feeling the emotion behind whatever word they have chosen). Act out the feeling together as a class.
- Pretend that *Stubborn* just walked into the room.
- Ask: What is one thing that *Stubborn* might be doing? Not saying, but doing—an action.
- Indicate that we are going to be writing in third person, beginning with *He, She,* or *It.* (Choose one.)
- Ask students to describe how he, she, or it might be acting.
- An action statement would look like this: *Stubborn came in and planted her feet and crossed her arms.*
- Remind students that this is Version 1, and that we will have an opportunity to revise later.

Slide 12

- Add a second action statement.
- Your action statement will look something like this: *She narrowed her eyes and pinched up her mouth and growled.*

Slide 13

- Ask: If *Stubborn* were an animal, what kind of animal would it be? Why, or under what circumstances?

- Expect about 90% of the class to say, "A donkey!" Push them a little harder. What other animals might act or appear to be stubborn?

- Remember that we always want to steer writers away from using clichés.

- Note that some possible examples might include a horse that won't jump, a dog that doesn't want to be put in its crate, a cat that doesn't want to be put in a bath.

- Entertain lots of suggestions. Assure students that there is no right or wrong answer, as long as the student can explain the logic behind the idea.

- Add your third line. Your draft may now look something like this.

Slide 14

- Put some color into the poem.
  - Is this word standing out like neon orange?
  - Does it have a red face or ears purple as an eggplant?
  - Is it wearing a black cape?

- Entertain lots of suggestions. If someone offers an off-the-wall idea, don't discount it. Instead ask for the student's reasoning. There are no right or wrong answers.

- Encourage writers to say *yellow as this*, *blue as that*, and so on.

- Add a fourth line. Your poem draft will now look something like this.

Slide 15

- Ask: What would *Stubborn* NOT do? Just as *Shy* would not be standing on a chair or belting out a song, what would *Stubborn* never do?

- Entertain several suggestions and choose one.

- Add a fifth line. Your draft will now look something like this.

Slide 16

- Add a sixth and final line. One more action.

- Your poem draft will now look something like this.

- Introduce this as the model the students will follow to write their own poems.

Time to Write

Slide 17

- Ask students to get out their writing notebooks, tablets, or computers.
- Check to make sure those using a notebook are open to a clean, two-page spread.
- Ask students to choose one feeling or state of being to write about.
- Click back to Slide 10 for some ideas.
- Explain to writers that they should not be confined to this list. It is not designed to hold them back; it is designed to get them started as they begin to think about their own ideas.
- Have writers put the feeling that they will be writing about at the top of the page.
- Remind writers that we are picking a word that captures an emotion, not a thing (tables, chairs, electron microscopes, etc.).

Slide 18

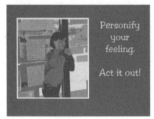

- Invite students to stand and try on the feeling they have jotted down.
- Have students act it out.
- Instruct students to personify the word.
- Coach them to notice what they are doing with their hands and their feet. Facial expressions. Shoulders. Hips.
- Remind them that this is research!

Time to Write

Slide 19

- Have students sit back down.
- Tell them that they have acted out the first line of their poem.
- Remind them that they are writing in third person. (We are personifying the word.)
- Ask: When you were personifying your word, what is one thing that your word was doing?

Slide 20

- Refer to the model poem.
- Note that the first line is an action.
- Walk students through the model one line at a time as they write their individual pieces.

Slide 21

- Work on the second line, which describes another action.
- Tell students that this could be a noise or another sensory observation.
- Instruct students to aim for at least two actions.
- Note that in this model poem, we actually have six actions.
- Inform writers that they may want to include more than two actions in these first two lines.

Slide 22

- Have students compare their word to an animal in the third line.
- Steer students away from saying something like "It is like a dog."
- Explain that there is a big difference between a growling dog and a sleeping dog. Same with a koala and a grizzly bear.
- Challenge students to be specific. Ask: An animal under what circumstances? (A monkey taking a nap or a monkey tearing through a basket of bananas?)

Slide 23

- Color your poem!
- Note that in our model, Stubborn's ears are purple.
- Ask: Was the writer's word *sparkly* like silver glitter? Was it dull gray and fading into the corners?
- Get students thinking with some additional questions:
  - Not just green . . . but green as what? Neon green like a traffic light or green like an army uniform?
- Remind students to be specific.
- Ask: Green as what? Blue as what?

Slide 24

- Turn the tables!
- Ask: What would your word *not* do? Never. Not a chance.
- Explain that this is an action line, even if the line is just *Jittery was just not sitting still.*

Slide 25

- One more action.
- Use *instead* for a transition word, or think of another transition word.
- Invite writers to add one or two more actions (or maybe more!).
- Note: We are contrasting line five.
- Don't duplicate anything from the first two lines.

Share

Slide 26

- Ask everyone to read their Version 1s at the same time. A seat symphony!
- Ask writers to then work with a partner or in a small group to share what they have so far.
- Ask to hear a couple out loud.
- Reinforce that what makes personification work are the specific examples the writers use to create a visual image for their readers—the evidence, not just the opinions.

Slide 27

- Note: Sara and Michael are the authors of many books of poetry and they are admitting here that they never get it right the first time.
- Note: This is true for all writers.

Time to Revise

Slide 28

- Ask students to turn back to the model poem.
- Explain to students that they are going to analyze this poem and lose the words they do not need.
- Warn them that we are about to get ruthless!
- Explain that they may also do some rearranging of individual lines.
- Begin with Line 1.
- Ask: What words do we *not* need here?
- Note that we have provided some ideas about how we may revise the poem personifying *Stubborn*.
- Use the poem you created together as a class as a model for revision.

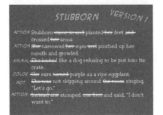

Slide 29

- Edit out unnecessary words.
- Note that when you get to the line referencing an animal, you can look at it two ways:
  - If you leave it as "like a dog refusing to be put into its crate," that is a simile.
  - If you take out the word *like*, it becomes a metaphor.
- Invite students to offer some substitutions.

Slide 30

- Here is Version 2 copied over.

- Note that in Version 1, we used the word *her* four times. In the revision, we use it only once.

- Point out that there is a similar problem with the word *and*. These are the types of things students will be looking to edit out of their own poems.

- Explain to students that it is now beginning to read more like a poem.

- Tell students that even though it's getting closer, we don't have to be done there.

- Suggest that they can bust up the lines and put them in a different order.

Slide 31

- Ask students to scan their poem drafts.

- Ask them to put a number 1 next to the line that they would like to be the first line of their final version.

- Expect that many students will say, "I like it just the way it is."

- Encourage students to take some risks and experiment.

Slide 32

- Show students what Version 3 of the Stubborn poem looks like, and point out how it reads differently with just a couple of changes in punctuation.

- Read through the poem again and have students see that it is okay to experiment and rearrange things.

- Note that we are reading this poem aloud several times as part of our revision process.

- Suggest that they do the same. Many times we can hear a mistake in our writing that we can't see on the page. Encourage mumbling!

- Ask students to make a Version 3 of their poem.

- Have them copy it over to a clean sheet of paper or key it into their computers. It is probably looking like an unreadable mess at this point.

- Tell them that even Version 3 may not be the final version of their poems.

- Suggest that they may wish to make a Version 4, 5, or even 24.

Share

Slide 33

- Ask students to share their final versions with a partner.

- Ask students to share with the class.

Slide 34: Take Away

- Emphasize that personification—using physical evidence to describe a feeling or emotion—can make our writing come alive.

- Remind students that poetry isn't the only place where they will find personification.

- Encourage students to keep their eyes open for examples of personification while they are reading nonfiction, sports reports, or fiction, and in everyday conversations.

Bonus Poems and Lesson Extensions

Slide 35

- These bonus poems have been selected to give you the opportunity to differentiate according to the needs of your classroom and to extend and reinforce the lesson.

Slide 36: "Do They Know?" by Amy Ludwig VanDerwater

- Read the poem aloud, have a student read it, and/or play the audio.

- Ask students to turn and talk to identify the clues that Amy provides to indicate personification. (Shake out their hair.)

- Ask: What else do you notice about this poem? (It is a concrete poem, or a shape poem.)

- Provide students with some background information about the poet:
  - Amy Ludwig VanDerwater is a writer and teacher living on Heart Rock Farm (The Poem Farm) in Holland, New York. For more information about her, please visit her ever-dynamic website: www.poemfarm.amylv.com.

Slide 37: "Sorry" by Sara Holbrook

- Read the poem aloud, have a student read it, and/or play the audio.

- Ask: Have you felt like you should apologize for something that you did, but you put it off? (This is a universal feeling.)

- Ask: What kind of comparison is it when the poet uses the word *like*? (A simile.)

- Ask students to read the first two lines of the poem and drop the word *like*.

- What kind of a comparison is it now? (A metaphor.)

Slide 38: "Line Breaks" by Pam Muñoz Ryan

- Read the poem aloud, have a student read it, and/or play the audio.

- Ask: What is going on between the adjective and the noun? (They are in love.)

- Ask: Why don't we want to separate them with a line break? (Because it would be pulling apart a kissing couple.)

- Provide students with some background information about the poet:

  - Pam Muñoz Ryan is mostly known for her award-winning picture books and novels. Like many writers, she also appreciates and writes poetry. For more information about Pam, her rich novels and fabulous picture books, as well as contact information, visit her website: www .pammunozryan.com.

Slide 39: "The Children's Auction" by Charles Mackay

- Ask: What words has Mackay personified in this poem? (*Pest, Famine, Fever, Beggary, Crime.*)

- Note: This is excerpted from a longer poem. You may want to review it before sharing it, as it may be a bit strong for younger students. The complete poem can be found at www.bartleby.com/71/1315.html.

- Provide students with some background information about the poet:

  - Charles Mackay (1814–1888) was a Scottish poet. As historical reference, you may wish to note that in the time that Mackay was writing, there were no safety nets for orphaned or poor children. Children who had no parents were on their own. This poem was originally published in 1915, in an anthology edited by Upton Sinclair, *The Cry for Justice: An Anthology of the Literature of Social Protest.*

ASSESSMENT

Here we provide a rubric you may choose to use. We provide this as a guide knowing that you may have other goals for your class. Don't feel compelled to assess every skill mentioned in this chart. We have had more success when we zero in on a skill or two with a lesson, but we want to afford you multiple options with these clinics.

Skill	3	2	1
Careful Reading	Demonstrates an understanding of how to use physical evidence to define an emotion in visual language.	Partially demonstrates an understanding of how to use physical evidence to define an emotion in visual language. May confuse more nuanced references.	Does not demonstrate an understanding of how to use physical evidence to define an emotion in visual language. Cannot see past literal meaning of text.
Structure and Organization	Demonstrates the ability to recognize and re-create a writing structure and to revise for concision and order.	Partially demonstrates the ability to recognize and re-create a writing structure. May not be able to complete one or two of the sequential steps or instructions.	Does not demonstrate the ability to recognize and re-create a writing structure. Is unable to follow most of the sequence and instructions.
Grammar Conventions	Demonstrates an understanding of how to maintain third person throughout the piece. Maintains subject-verb agreement throughout.	Partially demonstrates an understanding of how to maintain third person throughout the piece. Maintains subject-verb agreement most of the time.	Does not demonstrate the ability to maintain third person throughout the piece. Confuses subject-verb agreement throughout.
Connotative Word Meaning	Demonstrates an understanding of figurative language, word relationships, and nuances in word meanings when using personification.	Occasionally demonstrates an understanding of figurative language, word relationships, and nuances in word meanings when using personification. May have trouble articulating responses to one or two of the writing prompts.	Does not demonstrate an understanding of figurative language, word relationships, and nuances in word meanings when using personification. Cannot articulate responses to any of the writing prompts.
Speaking Skills	Consistently demonstrates effective presentation skills using good voice projection, inflection, pacing, eye contact, and stance.	Partially demonstrates effective presentation skills using good voice projection, inflection, pacing, eye contact, and stance.	Does not demonstrate effective presentation skills using good voice projection, inflection, pacing, eye contact, and stance.
Listening Skills	Actively participates in discussions about other students' work and is tuned in to student presentations.	Occasionally participates in discussions about other students' work and is tuned in to student presentations.	Does not participate in discussions about other students' work and is not tuned in to student presentations.

11

Point of View

WHY TEACH THIS?

You never really understand a person until you consider things from his point of view—until you climb into his skin and walk around in it.

—Atticus Finch in *To Kill a Mockingbird*, by Harper Lee

Making personal connections is a long-established comprehension strategy. Whether we are connecting with fiction, historical figures and events, scientific principles, or repurposing mathematical equations for our own practical applications, making a personal connection to knowledge helps us understand, remember, and apply what we have learned.

An often-cited article coming out of Harvard, written to help students develop their own reading and comprehension strategies, recommends that students "take the information apart, look at its parts, and then try to put it back together again in language that is meaningful to them. The best way to determine that you've really gotten the point is to be able to state it in your own words." According to Stephanie Harvey and Anne Goudvis, "Kids need an arsenal of tools to think deeply about text." We concur! Consider this clinic another fixture in your arsenal.

One way we can make these connections to subject matter is to try to see the world through the subject's perspective. Visualizing (another comprehension strategy) how another person, or thing, experiences the world gives us insight into our reading and writing. Similar to personification, writing from another's point of view causes us to think more deeply about the topic.

This clinic is designed to encourage students to figuratively walk a mile in another's shoes. Whether that "other" is a character from literature or a peptic enzyme, trying on an outside-of-self point of view will help our students form meaningful connections in their reading and writing.

Michael: Practicing writing from another's perspective will also enable our students to write stronger persuasive writing.

Sara: Changing our perspective builds empathy in the writer. It is much harder to ignore something or someone (a homeless person, an endangered pink dolphin, a volatile chemical element) if a writer has taken time to look at the world through their eyes.

Reference

Gilroy, S. (2004). *Interrogating Texts: 6 Reading Habits to Develop in Your First Year at Harvard.* Retrieved from http://isites.harvard.edu/fs/docs/icb.topic33378.files/interrogatingtexts.pdf

Harvey, S., & Goudvis, A. *(2013).* Comprehension at the Core. *The Reading Teacher, 66,* 432–439. doi:10.1002/TRTR.1145

CCSS AND CORRESPONDING ANCHOR STANDARDS

- **Cite** textual evidence to support analysis of what the text says explicitly as well as inferences drawn from the text.

  [4.RL.1] [5.RL.1] [6.RL.1] [7.RL.1] [8.RL.1]

- **Determine** the meaning of words and phrases as they are used in a text including figurative and cognitive meanings; analyze the impact of a specific word choice on meaning and tone.

  [4.RL.4] [5.RL.4] [6.RL.4] [7.RL.4] [8.RL.4]

- **Assess** how point of view or purpose shapes the content and style of a text.

  [4.RL.6] [5.RL.6] [6.RL.6] [7.RL.6] [8.RL.6]

- **Demonstrate** understanding of figurative language, word relationships, and nuances in word meanings.

  [4.L.5] [5.L.5] [6.L.5] [7.L.5] [8.L.5]

- **Read** and comprehend complex literary and informational texts independently and proficiently.

  [4.RL.10] [5.RL.10] [6.RL.10] [7.RL.10] [8.RL.10]

- **Determine** the meaning of words and phrases as they are used in text, including technical, connotative, and figurative meanings, and analyze how specific word choices shape meaning or tone.

  [4.RIT.4] [5.RIT.4] [6.RIT.4] [7.RIT.4] [8.RIT.4]

- **Write** informative/explanatory texts to examine a topic, convey ideas, concepts, and information through the selection, organization, and analysis of relevant content.

  [4.W.2] [5.W.2] [6.W.2] [7.W.2] [8.W.2]

- **Write** narrative to develop real or imagined experiences or events using effective technique, well-chosen details, and well-structured sequences.

  [4.W.3] [5.W.3] [6.W.3] [7.W.3] [8.W.3]

- **Produce** clear and coherent writing in which the development, organization, and style are appropriate to task, purpose, and audience.

  [4.W.4] [5.W.4] [6.W.4] [7.W.4] [8.W.4]

PRIOR TO THE LESSON

- Read through the entire lesson and review the slideshow to familiarize yourself with the clinic.

- Note that one of the bonus poems at the end of this clinic may be better suited to use as a model for your class than the one embedded in the clinic. Select the poem that works best for you and your students—your choice.

- Set up a separate surface (chart paper or white board) on which to compose a poem written collectively by you and your students.

THE LESSON

Slide 1

- Introduce the teaching poets by name (Sara and Michael), as they will appear throughout this lesson.

Slide 2

- Note: This picture was taken in Egypt at Edfu Temple.

Slide 3

- Ask: What does "point of view" mean? (The perspective of the narrator or speaker in a text.)
- Ask: How does one come to their point of view? (It's personal! Everyone and everything has its own point of view.)
- Ask: Can't there be differing points of view on the same subject? (Absolutely!)

Text Talk

Slide 4: "If I Were a Gear" by Michael Salinger

- Read the poem aloud, have a student read it, and/or play the audio.
- Have students turn and talk about the content of the poem.
- Ask them to quickly identify some true facts about how a gear behaves.
- Ask them to look at the structure of the poem.
- How many times did the author (Michael Salinger) use the phrase *If I were*?
- Note: He did not use it on every line.
- Note that the point of view is consistent throughout the poem; it's written in the first person from the perspective of a gear.

Slide 5

- Writing works like gears.
- First we have an experience—something we have seen, heard, or felt firsthand, or something we have heard about or know about from research.
- Explain that it could be that our experience is strictly something we have seen in our heads, such as science fiction, a dream, or a fantasy.

Slide 6

- Explain: Next we choose the words and the genre to communicate our experience.
- We can choose to write a speech, a letter, a story, a poem—there are many choices we have as writers.
- We also choose which words we will use, what best describes our experience.

Slide 7

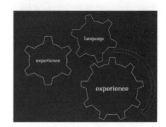

- Finally, we are able to communicate our experience to another person.
- Note: The words we choose and the form in which we put those words are crucial.
- This is how we communicate ideas and make ourselves understood.

Work Together

Slide 8

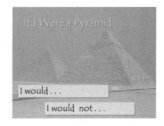

- Announce that you will be writing a poem from the point of view of a pyramid. (Note: You may wish to choose another topic from your current unit of study.)
- Ask students to brainstorm at least three to five things that they would or would not be able to do if they were a pyramid. If students don't have enough knowledge about the topic, they may want to consult research sources to gather details.
- Observations may include:
  - shape
  - function
  - location
  - construction materials
  - size
- Use this brainstorm to compose a poem together.
- Arrange the lines for rhythm and emphasis.
- Ask students to include at least one observation of what a pyramid would not do.

Slide 9

- Here is a picture of a camel and a camel rider beside a pyramid.
- Ask students to turn and talk about how a poem titled "If I Were a Camel Rider" would differ from "If I Were a Camel."
- Ask: How might they differ in their point of view about (for example) that stick?
- Reinforce the idea that our experience is different depending on our point of view.
- Remind writers that we can choose our point of view when we write.
- Explain that we choose one point of view when we write, unless we are writing a conversation.

Time to Write

Slide 10

- Ask students to get out their writer's notebooks, paper, or computers.
- Explain that they will be writing from a point of view other than their own.
- Consider writing prompts that are rooted the content areas. For instance:
  - *If I were a migrant in the 19th century*
  - *If I were an esophagus, a Conestoga wagon, or a circle*
- Have research options available (the Internet, dictionaries, texts).

Slide 11

- Have students divide their papers as shown in the slide.
- Have the writers brainstorm by using research materials, thinking about their experience, and conferring with others.
- Brainstorm for about 10 minutes.
- Use the right column to write the poem.
- Have everyone read through their Version 1s aloud at the same time. Seat symphony!

Time to Revise

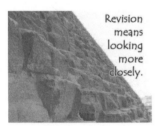

Slide 12

- Ask students to look up from their writing to reexamine the class poem.
- Remind them that this is just Version 1.
- Read through Version 1 again.
- Invite students to offer ideas, line by line, on how they might edit the poem to get rid of some of the repetition and sharpen the piece.
- Don't spend too much time on this. You are simply modeling the process that students will follow in their own revisions.

Slide 13

- Begin the revision process by having students partner up to read their poems to one another.
- Ask students to discuss their Version 1 with their partners and work together to revise their pieces.
- Conferring with partners may give the writers more and better ideas to incorporate into their revised piece.
- Remind students that they may wish to do the following:
  - Delete some of the repeated lines.
  - Use a refrain line.

- Develop a strong lead.
- Develop a strong conclusion.
- Change or break a pattern in the poem for greater emphasis.
- Give students about 5–7 minutes for revision.
- Have students make a clean copy of their poems in their notebooks or on their computers or pads.

Share

Slide 14

- Have individual students share their poems with the class (as many as time permits).
- Ask: What did you learn by taking another point of view other than your own?
- Ask the listening audience what they learned by hearing a poem from an alternative point of view.

Slide 15

- Reiterate that the world looks different when we change our point of view.

Bonus Poems and Lesson Extensions

Slide 16

- These bonus poems have been selected to give you the opportunity to differentiate according to the needs of your classroom and to extend and reinforce the lesson.

Slide 17: "Mary Todd Lincoln Speaks of Her Son's Death, 1862" by Paul Janeczko

- Read the poem aloud, have a student read it, and/or play the audio.
- Ask: Who is speaking in this poem? (Mary Todd Lincoln.)
- Ask: What has happened? (Her son Willie has died.)
- Note: In order to write this poem, the poet had to stand in the shoes of the speaker of the poem.
- Ask: How can a poet do this? (Research.)
- Let this poem be a springboard for students to research and write their own persona poems.

- Provide students with some background information on the author:
  - Paul Janeczko is a former teacher and an esteemed poet. To read more poems he has written in the voices of others, check out his book *Requiem: Poems of the Terezin Ghetto* (Candlewick Press). For more ideas about the reading of poetry, refer to *Reading Poetry* (Heinemann). These are just two of his many titles; you can find out more, in addition to information about his work with teachers and school visits, by visiting www.paulbjaneczko.com.

Slides 18–19: "If I Were a Poem" by Sara Holbrook

- Read the poem aloud, have a student read it, and/or play audio (on Slide 19).
- Note: This is four verses of a five-verse poem. Sara thought the entire text of the original poem might be too strong for younger readers. The full text of the poem can be found online.

Slide 20

- Dig up more information about the excavation at Jamestown by visiting http://anthropology.si.edu/writteninbone.
- For more information about Sally Walker and her amazing book, visit www.sallymwalker.com.

Slide 21: "Remember Me" by Sara Holbrook

- Read the poem aloud, have a student read it, and/or play audio (on the next slide).
- Explain to students that Sara began writing this poem by imagining, *If I were a 15-year-old boy in Jamestown . . .*
- Sara researched *Written in Bone*, other sources available through the Smithsonian, and other literature from that time period (in order to get the language right).

Slide 22

- Ask: Where is it evident that the author did research? (In the details from the boy's story and in the language.)
- Ask: How does this 15-year-old boy's desire to appear brave align with the attitudes of today's teens? (No one wants to be seen as weak.)
- Note: The form of this poem is a sonnet, which was a common poetry form in the days of early Jamestown.

ASSESSMENT

Here we provide a rubric you may choose to use. We provide this as a guide knowing that you may have other goals for your class. Don't feel compelled to assess every skill mentioned in this chart. We have had more success when we zero in on a skill or two with a lesson, but we want to afford you multiple options with these clinics.

Skill	3	2	1
Careful Reading	Demonstrates an understanding of the impact point of view has on the context and meaning of a piece of writing. Is able to infer meaning from text that is written from an alternative point of view.	Partially demonstrates an understanding of the impact point of view has on the context and meaning of a piece of writing. Is inconsistent in ability to infer meaning from text that is written from an alternative point of view.	Is unable to infer meaning from text that is written from an alternative point of view. Cannot empathize with the voice of the text.
Structure and Organization	Demonstrates the ability to recognize and re-create a writing structure. Maintains a consistent and logical voice.	Partially demonstrates the ability to recognize and re-create a writing structure. Maintains a consistent and logical voice. May write something that seems inconsistent with the point of view being taken.	Does not demonstrate the ability to articulate another's point of view.
Textual Evidence to Support Voice of Writing	Demonstrates an understanding of subject matter through accurate interpretation of facts obtained through research and experience. Is able to articulate findings through a consistent alternative point of view.	Partially demonstrates an understanding of subject matter. May misinterpret a fact or two, or may fail to maintain a consistent alternative point of view.	Is unable to articulate an understanding of subject matter or to write from an alternative point of view.
Connotative Word Meaning	Demonstrates the ability to write from an imagined point of view. Remains consistent, using a convincing voice throughout.	Occasionally demonstrates the ability to write from an imagined point of view. May be inconsistent in maintaining a convincing voice.	Does not demonstrate the ability to write from an imagined point of view.
Speaking Skills	Consistently demonstrates effective presentation skills using good voice projection, inflection, pacing, eye contact, and stance.	Partially demonstrates effective presentation skills using good voice projection, inflection, pacing, eye contact, and stance.	Does not demonstrate effective presentation skills using good voice projection, inflection, pacing, eye contact, and stance.
Listening Skills	Actively participates in discussions about other students' work and is tuned in to student presentations.	Occasionally participates in discussions about other students' work and is tuned in to student presentations.	Does not participate in discussions about other students' work and is not tuned in to student presentations.

12

Word Definition Poems

WHY TEACH THIS?

"*Hope* is a feathery thing. . . ." So says Emily Dickinson. Of course, for your average marginally prepared middle schooler, *hope* may be the chance that the class bell will ring before being called on. Just as importantly though, is: What is *hope* not? A pie in the face? A door slamming? Imagining different possibilities causes us to think deeply about a word, helping that word become meaningful and memorable.

Poetry is often used to define emotions, events, ideas, slivers of time, and—in the case of this writing clinic—words. Whether these are big idea words, such as *respect, family, betrayal,* or content area vocabulary words, such as *igneous, simile, taxation,* having students collaboratively write about these terms will help them deepen their understanding of words they already know and use as well as learn new terminology in a memorable way.

The graphic organizer and the composition prompts in this clinic will encourage your students to engage in multilayered reasoning as they come to understand both the new and the familiar vocabulary they encounter. Students will embed these terms in their writing and surround them with language and meaning that is authentic to their own understanding. The resultant poems will be easy to assess and will be far more objective artifacts of learning than those generated in response to the old *look up a word and use it in a sentence* method that so many of us suffered through as students and instructors.

Michael: That's not exactly what Emily Dickinson said.

Sara: It's as close as we can get without violating copyright laws.

CCSS AND CORRESPONDING ANCHOR STANDARDS

- **Demonstrate** understanding of figurative language, word relationships, and nuances in word meanings.

  [4.L.5] [5.L.5] [6.L.5] [7.L.5] [8.L.5]

- **Interpret** words and phrases as they are used in a text, including determining technical, connotative, and figurative meanings, and analyze how specific word choices shape meaning or tone.

  [4.RL.4] [5.RL.4] [6.RL.4] [7.RL.4] [8.RL.4]

- **Analyze** the structure of texts, including how specific sentences, paragraphs, and larger portions of the text (e.g., a section, chapter, scene, or stanza) relate to each other and the whole.

  [4.RL.5] [5.RL.5] [6.RL.5] [7.RL.5] [8.RL.5]

- **Read** and comprehend complex literary and informational texts independently and proficiently.

  [4.RL.10] [5.RL.10] [6.RL.10] [7.RL.10] [8.RL.10]

- **Write** informative/explanatory texts to examine and convey complex ideas and information clearly and accurately through the effective selection, organization, and analysis of content.

  [4.W.2] [5.W.2] [6.W.2] [7.W.2] [8.W.2]

- **Write** narrative to develop real or imagined experiences or events using effective technique, well-chosen details, and well-structured sequences.

  [4.W.3] [5.W.3] [6.W.3] [7.W.3] [8.W.3]

- **Produce** clear and coherent writing in which the development, organization, and style are appropriate to task, purpose, and audience.

  [4.W.4] [5.W.4] [6.W.4] [7.W.4] [8.W.4]

- **Demonstrate** command of the conventions of standard English grammar and usage when writing or speaking.

  [4.L.1] [5.L.1] [6.L.1] [7.L.1] [8.L.1]

PRIOR TO THE LESSON

- Read through the entire lesson and review the slideshow to familiarize yourself with the clinic.

- Note that one of the bonus poems at the end of this clinic may be better suited to use as a model for your class than the one embedded in the clinic. Select the poem that works best for you and your students—your choice.

- Set up a separate surface (chart paper or white board) on which to compose a poem written collectively by you and your students.

THE LESSON

Slide 1

- Introduce the teaching poets by name (Sara and Michael), as they will appear throughout this lesson.

Slides 2–3

- Explain that we are going to take a closer look at words and discuss, research, and write poems about word meanings.

Slide 4

- Discuss the different strategies commonly used to assign meaning when encountering a new word.

Slide 5

- Ask: What are some of the pitfalls to context clues? (If one doesn't know the meanings of the words around the new term, context won't help—even if the word is used in what looks to be a grammatically correct sentence.)

Slide 6

- Note that this sentence is grammatically correct. Ask: Why, then, doesn't it make sense? ("That woman cannot stand on one oxter.")

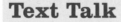

Slide 7

- Urge students to look deeper than context clues in order to be sure of what a word means.
- This is also a problem when we rely on a thesaurus without doing any follow-up research on the word we have discovered there.

Text Talk

Slide 8: "Jinx" by Michael Salinger

- Read the poem aloud, have a student read it, and/or play the audio.
- Discuss the piece with the class.
- Ask: What is the word *Jinx* not? (It is not good luck.)
- Ask: What does Jinx do? (Make things worse.)

Slide 9

- Ask: What does *subtle* not mean? What is it not like?

- Ask: How does explaining what the word does not mean help define the word *subtle*? (Because it follows logic, but is just novel enough to pique our attention.)

Work Together

Slide 10

- Time to write together as a group.

- Let the students have a say in which word you will define in a poem.

- Choose from a current unit of study, a piece of fiction or nonfiction reading, your word wall, etc.

- Prepare to move to a blank surface (white board or chart paper) to complete your group write (model poem).

Slide 11

- Ask for volunteers to tell you what your word does.

- Ask: What does it sound, taste, smell, or feel like?

- Suggest that writers take their word for a walk.

- Ask: How would your word behave in the cafeteria or on a soccer field?

- Ask: Now, what would the word not do?

- Complete a couple of examples in the top box (does) and then move to the bottom box (doesn't).

- Skip back and forth between the top and bottom boxes, brainstorming for 5 minutes or so.

- See the next slide for a sample completed cheat sheet.

- Note: We call this a "cheat sheet" because we want the kids to go back and swipe ideas from it. It's a bit of a ruse. We notice that kids often forget to use their brainstorms when they finally get down to writing.

Slide 12

- This is a sample cheat sheet we completed using the word *friendship*.

- Leave this sample up while you complete your group write.

- Keep referring back to it as a model of what is meant by "be specific."

- Don't hesitate to push students by urging them to be more specific.

Slide 13

- Remember, we call this a "cheat sheet" to encourage students to steal from their own brainstorms.

- Reinforce that writers don't ignore all the work in their brainstorms when they start to write. Often when kids start to write, they ignore all the work in their brainstorm.
- To begin writing your poem, just steal one of the idea seeds and plant it on the right side of the page.

Slide 14

- Encourage that first planted seed to grow through the use of transition words. (On the slide are some examples of transition words.)
- Ask if the writers can think of more.
- Continue to compose your poem, using four or five of the idea seeds.
- End the poem with a simple statement of fact. There is no transition word needed in this last line. (Breaks the pattern.)
- Remember, it's okay to come up with new ideas as you write together, but don't let the students neglect their brainstorm.
- Leave this finished group write on display as a model poem for students to reference as they begin to write their own.

Time to Write

Slide 15

- Have students partner up so they can discuss their word.
- Ask each pair to choose one word to write about.
- Keep in mind that the brainstorm is collaborative. When it comes time to compose their poems, students will have the option to write on their own.
- Have students get out their notebooks or paper.
- Note: We have found that the brainstorm portion of this clinic works best with paper and pencil rather than with a computer or tablet.

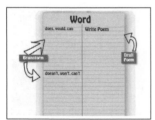

Slide 16

- Have students divide their papers like this.
- Have them brainstorm to complete their cheat sheet.
- Draw from research materials, their experience, and by conferring with their partners.
- Brainstorm for maybe 10 minutes.
- This is a lively portion of the clinic; everyone will be talking.
- Circulate about the room, reminding students to include specifics and not generalizations.
- Announce to students that now that the brainstorm is complete, it is time to draft a poem.

- Give students the option of writing the poem either with their partner (two authors, one poem) or on their own.
- Whichever they decide, all participants will need a copy of the work.

Slide 17

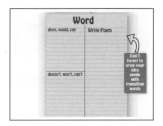

- Remind: Don't forget to grow your ideas with transition words.
- Ask your students to include at least one true-life example if they can. For example, a friend should not be described as "having one's back," rather note that a friend would lend you lunch money or back up an excuse to a parent.

Share

Slide 18

- Have all of the students read their poems aloud at the same time. Seat symphony!
- Ask students to take turns sharing their poems with the class.
- Spark a brief discussion after each poem by asking: Now, what does this word mean? What does it not mean?
- Take this opportunity to correct misconceptions if they arise. (They will.)

Slide 19

- Take away: A word can be defined by what it means and what it does not mean.

Bonus Poems and Lesson Extensions

Slide 20

- These bonus poems have been selected to give you the opportunity to differentiate according to the needs of your classroom and to extend and reinforce the lesson.
- Countless poets have written poems to define words.
- Explain that some poets embed definitions in longer poems.
- Let students know that once we have learned how to creatively define a word in the context of our writing, we can use this skill in a variety of ways.
- Note: We have included more bonus poems in this clinic; choose those that best fit your classroom reading levels.

Slide 21: "Love" by Sara Holbrook

- Read the poem aloud, have a student read it, and/or play the audio.
- Ask: What specific details does Sara cite?
- Notice she does not say, "Love has my back" or "Is there for me."

Slide 22: "It Was a Beauty That I Saw" by Ben Jonson

- Read the poem aloud, have a student read it, and/or play the audio.

- Inform students that this poem was written in 1629.

- Ask: What is Jonson saying about beauty here?

- Note: This is an excerpt from a longer poem, which you may wish to share.

- Familiarize students with Ben Jonson:

  ○ He was a contemporary of William Shakespeare and a bigwig in the 17th century literary scene.

  ○ He was a poet, a playwright, and an actor.

Slide 23: "Democracy" by Sara Holbrook

- Read the poem aloud, have a student read it, and/or play the audio.

- Notice that this piece is composed entirely of *nots* until the middle of the piece, where that pattern is broken.

- Point out to students that the pattern in this poem was broken well before the ending.

- Note that it might be fun to extend this lesson with Carl Sandburg's poem "Muckers," which you can find at www.bartleby.com/165/18.html.

Slide 24: "Novice" by Michael Salinger

- Ask: How does Michael define *novice*? (As someone who doesn't have much experience.)

- Ask: What is a novice? (Someone just starting out.)

- Ask: What is it not? (It's not someone you want doing surgery on you!)

Slide 25: "Tao Te Ching, #11" by Lao Tzu

- Read the poem aloud, have a student read it, and/or play the audio.

- Note: Poets have been writing for centuries, across continents, across cultures.

- Ask students to discuss how this poem reflects on the writing clinic they just did. (We find what is useful when we look at what is not there.)

- Provide students with some background information about the poet:

  ○ Lao Tzu (one of a variety of spellings in use), loosely translated as "old master," was a Chinese poet and philosopher. Much is available about him online.

ASSESSMENT

Here we provide a rubric you may choose to use. We provide this as a guide knowing that you may have other goals for your class. Don't feel compelled to assess every skill mentioned in this chart. We have had more success when we zero in on a skill or two with a lesson, but we want to afford you multiple options with these clinics.

Skill	3	2	1
Careful Reading	Demonstrates a deeper understanding of words through examining their relationships with other words, research, and common experience.	Partially demonstrates an understanding of word meanings. May not pick up on nuanced meanings and may display some misperceptions when trying to analyze text.	Does not demonstrate an understanding of word meanings and is unable to understand texts in which the words appear.
Structure and Organization	Demonstrates the ability to recognize and re-create a writing structure and to craft a strong conclusion. There is a well-developed pre-write and the finished piece uses transition words followed by the growth of relevant ideas.	Demonstrates a partial ability to recognize and re-create a writing structure and to craft a strong conclusion. The pre-write may be lacking and transitions may be followed by generalizations that do not add to understanding.	Does not demonstrate the ability to recognize and re-create a writing structure. The piece may not be complete and there may be gross misperceptions regarding word meanings.
Write Informative Explanatory Text	Demonstrates the use of well-researched details and specific examples in support of their word definitions.	Partially demonstrates the use of research, details, and some examples to support their word definitions. May include some clichés or unsupported interpretations.	Demonstrates no apparent research. Shows misperceptions in the meaning of the words. Uses no transitions or follows transitions with nonsequiturs.
Speaking Skills	Consistently demonstrates effective presentation skills using good voice projection, inflection, pacing, eye contact, and stance.	Partially demonstrates effective presentation skills using good voice projection, inflection, pacing, eye contact, and stance.	Does not demonstrate effective presentation skills using good voice projection, inflection, pacing, eye contact, and stance.
Listening Skills	Actively participates in discussions about other students' work and is tuned in to student presentations.	Occasionally participates in discussions about other students' work and is tuned in to student presentations.	Does not participate in discussions about other students' work and is not tuned in to student presentations.

13

Weighting the Evidence

Logical Poetry

WHY TEACH THIS?

Do I cut the red wire first or do I cut the blue? Which is more important? The fact that guy coming at me is wearing a ball cap or that he is a zombie? Should I spend my last few dollars on brake fluid or an air freshener for my car?

Not all the decisions we are faced with in life are so dramatic. Still, the ability to weight any set of particulars in order of their significance is a crucial life skill, a skill that is grown slowly over time. This clinic is designed to lead students to evaluate the qualities of something so that they can make logical inferences.

Why is it so important that we work to build evaluative logic in students? In order to summarize, to develop an argument, to formulate an analysis, or to reach a logical conclusion, students must be able to look at a set of facts and put them in order of their importance. It is imperative in all fields, including science, mathematics, architecture, computer engineering, and literary analysis. In fact, we would be hard pressed to name a field where deductive logic is not important.

Michael: Directions from IKEA and poetry may seem completely unrelated at first look, but patterns, sequence, and concise language are traits that are transferable between these types of writing.

Sara: Weighing the importance of information is an essential life skill that extends well beyond school. We are always telling our kids to make wise choices. Well, being able to assess and evaluate information and place it in order of importance is how good decisions come to be made.

CCSS AND CORRESPONDING ANCHOR STANDARDS

- **Read** closely to determine what the text says explicitly and to make logical inferences from it; cite specific textual evidence when writing or speaking to support conclusions drawn from the text.

  [4.RL.1] [5.RL.1] [6.RL.1] [7.RL.1] [8.RL.1]

- **Interpret** words and phrases as they are used in a text, including determining technical, connotative, and figurative meanings, and analyze how specific word choices shape meaning or tone.

  [4.RL.4] [5.RL.4] [6.RL.4] [7.RL.4] [8.RL.4]

- **Demonstrate** understanding of figurative language, word relationships, and nuances in word meanings.

  [4.L.5] [5.L.5] [6.L.5] [7.L.5] [8.L.5]

- **Read** and comprehend complex literary and informational texts independently and proficiently.

  [4.RL.10] [5.RL.10] [6.RL.10] [7.RL.10] [8.RL.10]

- **Interpret** words and phrases as they are used in a text, including determining technical, connotative, and figurative meanings, and analyze how specific word choices shape meaning or tone.

  [4.RIT.4] [5.RIT.4] [6.RIT.4] [7.RIT.4] [8.RIT.4]

- **Write** informative/explanatory texts to examine and convey complex ideas and information clearly and accurately through the effective selection, organization, and analysis of content.

  [4.W.2] [5.W.2] [6.W.2] [7.W.2] [8.W.2]

- **Write** narrative to develop real or imagined experiences or events using effective technique, well-chosen details, and well-structured sequences.

  [4.W.3] [5.W.3] [6.W.3] [7.W.3] [8.W.3]

- **Produce** clear and coherent writing in which the development, organization, and style are appropriate to task, purpose, and audience.

  [4.W.4] [5.W.4] [6.W.4] [7.W.4] [8.W.4]

PRIOR TO THE LESSON

- Read through the entire lesson and review the slideshow to familiarize yourself with the clinic.

- Note that one of the bonus poems at the end of this clinic may be better suited to use as a model for your class than the one embedded in the clinic. Select the poem that works best for you and your students— your choice.

- Set up a separate surface (chart paper or white board) on which to compose a poem written collectively by you and your students.

- This clinic is presented in two parts—you may consider taking two class sessions to complete both.

THE LESSON

Slide 1

- Introduce the teaching poets by name (Sara and Michael), as they will appear throughout this lesson.

Slide 2

- Read or have a student read the text on the slide.
- Explain that we are going to estimate measurements and then use them to write a poem using percentages.
- Tell students they will also be using measurements to write a sequenced recipe poem.

Slide 3

- Note that all academic disciplines—from themes in literature, to trends in social or world studies, to concepts in math and science—involve measuring and evaluating the importance of qualities and ideas.
- Ask: Can you recall a time when a teacher asked you to identify the most important elements in a lesson or piece of text?
- Ask students to turn and talk to each other about the last time they were asked to determine what was greater than or less than.
- Have students think about these two questions as they discuss:
  - How did they do it?
  - Did they measure or estimate?

Text Talk

Slide 4

- Read the poem aloud, have a student read it, and/or play the audio.
- Ask: What do Sara's percentages have to add up to? (100%.)
- Point out that this poem has a strong conclusion that breaks the pattern of the poem.
- Ask: What does the conclusion do to the poem? (It sums things up.)

Slide 5

- Invite one enthusiastic volunteer to the front of the classroom.
- Write the class's observations about the enthusiastic volunteer on a white board or piece of chart paper.
- Instruct the class to work together to make a list of details about the volunteer.

Work Together

Slide 6

- Make a quick list of details about your enthusiastic volunteer using this as a model.

- See the slide for some examples of the kinds of details you are looking for. (This particular enthusiastic volunteer played the trumpet in the band and was a baseball fan.)

- Ask some questions of your volunteer (without getting too personal).

- Favorite food? Favorite sports? Siblings? Heritage?

- List at least 8–12 characteristics.

- Listing 20 characteristics will only slow you down here. You want to build a quick model and then let the students go on to write their own poems.

Slide 7

- Give some of the established details a weighted value using percentages.

- Ask: Which do you suppose is more important, the fact that he is wearing khaki shorts or that he is a brother?

- No need to assign percentages to every detail listed. You are simply modeling the method students will be using as they write their own poems.

- Remind students that when they do this on their own, their percentages must add up to 100%.

- Excuse your enthusiastic volunteer and have everyone give him or her a hand for being a good sport.

Time to Write

Slide 8

- Ask everyone to take out a sheet of paper or their writer's notebooks.

- Make sure students use a spreadsheet format if they are working on computers, so that it will be easier for them to add up the numbers.

- Instruct students to compose a personal list of characteristics.

- Leave this slide visible while students make their lists.

- Give students no more than 7–10 minutes to do this; a long list of characteristics is too much to handle.

- Suggest a minimum number of characteristics to avoid having students use just one. For example, usually we have one joker who will say something like, "I'm 100% skateboard. I'm done."

Slide 9

- Ask the writers to assign percentages to their selected attributes.
- Make sure this is done in pencil, because changes are part of the writing process.
- Give students about 8–10 minutes to complete this task.
- Note that some students will think of additional characteristics, particularly if they attempt a rhyming pattern.
- Encourage them to keep it real; for example, don't say you are 10% cat (even though it rhymes with baseball hat) if you are fiercely a dog person.
- Remember, these percentages need to add up to 100%.

Slide 10

- Ask students to check the order of their lines for rhythm and emphasis.
- Tell them that now is the time to move lines around if they wish.
- Ask students to bookend their percentage poem with a strong lead and a strong conclusion.
- Remind them that the leading and concluding lines should sum up the content of the poem.

Share

Slide 11

- Have students share their poem with a partner first.
- Instruct students to then read their poem aloud at the same time. Seat symphony!
- Ask for volunteers (enthusiasm optional) to read their poems to the class.
- Note that these poems may be illustrated, turned into a pie chart or bar graph, and posted/published.
- Consider having students write percentage poems about historical figures, fictional characters, sports heroes, etc.

Slide 12

- Here's another idea for a measurement poem that they can whip up in no time.

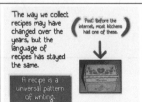

Slide 13

- Explain that the way we collect recipes may have changed over the years, but the language of recipes has stayed the same.
- Tell students that in this way, a recipe is a universal pattern of sequenced writing.

Text Talk

Slide 14: "Mountain Bike Soufflé" by Michael Salinger

- Read the poem aloud (three slides), have a student read it, and/or play the audio (on Slide 17).

Slide 15

- Slide two of three.
- See the entire poem on Slide 17.

Slide 16

- Slide three of three.
- See the entire poem on Slide 17.

Slide 17

- Encourage a closer reading by dividing the class into two groups.
- Ask half of the class to analyze the poem for recipe words.
- Have the other half look for bike terms.
- Confer!
- Discuss how Michael combined these two word lists into a recognizable pattern—a recipe. (Carefully observe the verb choices.)

Slide 18

- Establish that the sequence (recipe) that students write will lead to an outcome.
- Explain that the first step in writing a recipe poem is to select an outcome (i.e., to answer the question: What are we going to cook up?).
- See next slide for some ideas.

Work Together

Slide 19

- Establish an outcome for the recipe.
- IMPORTANT: We are looking for a non-food topic.
- Select one of these words or choose a word from your current unit of study.

- Remember that this is also a lesson in figurative language. You would lose that component of the clinic if you actually produced something edible.

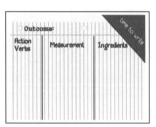

Slide 20

- Prepare three columns on a white board or chart paper.
- Label the columns Action Verbs (recipe oriented), Measurement (how much), and Ingredients.
- Have students brainstorm and volunteer four or five entries for each column.
- Write these suggestions on the white board, chart paper, or any place the entire class can see them.
- Note that we will probably not use all of them, but brainstorming will help to identify the best ideas.
- Combine the column entries to form a short poem.
- Refer back to Michael's poem (Slide 17) or consult a cookbook as a model.
- Do not go into too much depth here; you are simply modeling what the students will do next on their own.

Time to Write

Slide 21

- Prepare a piece of notebook paper as you see on the slide.
- Decide if students should work solo or in pairs, and then ask them to prepare a piece of notebook paper like this.
- Ask each student (or pair) to come up with an outcome: What is this a recipe for?
- Supply students with research materials such as cookbooks or online recipes, so they can find some good action verbs.
- Provide students with resources such as nonfiction texts, dictionaries, and other sources of relevant content area materials to enable students to create a detailed list of ingredients.
- For instance, if the recipe's outcome is metamorphic rock, you may want an earth science text handy.

Slide 22

- Time to mix your ideas into a poem now!
- Inform students that they may compose their poems in pairs or solo.
- Note that conversation will continue throughout the writing process as students look to one another to clarify ideas.

Share

Slide 23

- Have students share their work aloud simultaneously. Seat symphony!
- Ask students to share with a neighbor.
- Select enthusiastic volunteers to read to the class. (You may want to bribe them with a cookie for this one.)

Slide 24

- Explain that estimating the importance of details using measurement terms makes our writing (and thinking) more precise.

Bonus Poems and Lesson Extensions

Slide 25

- These bonus poems have been selected to give you the opportunity to differentiate according to the needs of your classroom and to extend and reinforce the lesson.

Slide 26: "Labels" by Sara Holbrook

- Read the poem aloud, have a student read it, and/or play the audio.
- Ask students to turn and talk about how this poem is similar to the poems they produced in the clinic and how it is different. ("Labels" doesn't use measurement terms.)
- Remember, with any recipe, one seasons to taste. We hope students will do the same in their writing and adapt strategies from these clinics to help them find their voices through poetry.

Slide 27: "Recipe for Unity" by Kelly Harris

- Read the poem aloud, have a student read it, and/or play the audio (on the next slide).

Slide 28

- Explain the basic premise of the poem as poet Kelly Harris setting a peaceful table.
- Ask: What is the outcome the poet is looking for? (Unity.)
- Ask: What are some of the ingredients she recommends? (Laughter, hope, smiles, celebration, etc.)

- Ask: What does she mean by "carry someone's feelings like an egg"? (Treat them with tenderness.)

- Ask: Does cool usually rise above heat? (No, heat rises.)

- Invite students to think about what the poet means by this. (Entertain ideas, no right or wrong answers.)

- Provide students with some background information about the poet:

  o Kelly Harris-DeBerry lives and writes in New Orleans, Louisiana, where she is the creator of Poems & Pink Ribbons, a poetry workshop for breast cancer patients, survivors, and their loved ones. She holds a Master of Fine Arts from Lesley University and is widely published. You can find out more about her at www.kellyharrispoetry.com.

Slide 29: "Recipe for Genocide" by Sara Holbrook

- Read the poem aloud, have a student read it, and/or play the audio.

- Point out that this piece relies heavily on recipe verbs—not so much on measurement or sequence.

- Encourage closer reading by having students reread the text while focusing on the poet's verb choices.

ASSESSMENT

Here we provide a rubric you may choose to use. We provide this as a guide knowing that you may have other goals for your class. Don't feel compelled to assess every skill mentioned in this chart. We have had more success when we zero in on a skill or two with a lesson, but we want to afford you multiple options with these clinics.

Skill	3	2	1
Careful Reading	Demonstrates an understanding of how a sequence of events and the relative importance of each lead to a logical outcome or conclusion. Recognizes all of the elements of a pattern sequence.	Partially demonstrates an understanding of how a sequence of events and the relative importance of each lead to a logical outcome or conclusion. May have trouble recognizing some of the elements of a pattern sequence.	Does not demonstrate an understanding of how a sequence of events and the relative importance of each lead to a logical outcome or conclusion. Cannot make meaning by connecting an abstract idea to a sequenced pattern of writing.
Structure and Organization	Demonstrates the ability to recognize and re-create a writing structure comprising measurements and logical sequence based on examples.	Partially demonstrates the ability to recognize and re-create a writing structure comprising measurements and logical sequence based on examples. May have trouble weighting an element or two or may have a misstep in the sequence.	Does not demonstrate the ability to recognize and re-create a writing structure comprising measurements and logical sequence based on examples. Is unable to re-create a recipe of an abstract idea or estimate relative importance of ingredients.
Write Informative Explanatory Texts	Creates a piece of writing that demonstrates understanding of the subject matter, including pertinent facts, appropriate weighting of details, and logical sequence.	Creates a piece of writing that demonstrates partial understanding of the subject matter. Some facts may be misrepresented or the weight of their importance may be skewed.	Creates a piece of writing that shows no basis in fact. Importance of components shows no concern for weighting of importance. Sequence is not logical.
Speaking Skills	Consistently demonstrates effective presentation skills using good voice projection, inflection, pacing, eye contact, and stance.	Partially demonstrates effective presentation skills using good voice projection, inflection, pacing, eye contact, and stance.	Does not demonstrate effective presentation skills using good voice projection, inflection, pacing, eye contact, and stance.
Listening Skills	Actively participates in discussions about other students' work and is tuned in to student presentations.	Occasionally participates in discussions about other students' work and is tuned in to student presentations.	Does not participate in discussions about other students' work and is not tuned in to student presentations.

14

The Prepositional Phrase Poem

WHY TEACH THIS?

"I just saw a monkey driving a pickup truck!"

What's the first question you would ask after hearing a statement like this?

"Where?!"

Number one, because you might want to avoid that particular stretch of road, and number two, because the setting is a crucial piece of the story.

Setting adds a sense of place-specific imagery that allows our audience to picture where the action is happening. There's a big difference between holding one's breath *in a theater* and holding one's breath *under the water*. Describing a setting does more than just add visual language to narratives; it provides context for fiction and nonfiction texts.

The intent behind this writing clinic is to help your students incorporate a sense of action, detail, and place into their writing through the use of prepositional phrases. Again, we will be setting up a pattern for students to use for their writing, which we will then encourage them to break at the very end of their poems.

Sara: It may only be a word or a phrase, but every poem has a setting that helps the audience picture the writer's vision.

Michael: Plus, prepositional phrase poems are a fun way to reteach this writing convention.

CCSS AND CORRESPONDING ANCHOR STANDARDS

- **Interpret** words and phrases as they are used in a text, including determining technical, connotative, and figurative meanings, and analyze how specific word choices shape meaning or tone.

  [4.RL.4] [5.RL.4] [6.RL.4] [7.RL.4] [8.RL.4]

- **Analyze** the structure of texts, including how specific sentences, paragraphs, and larger portions of the text (e.g., a section, chapter, scene, or stanza) relate to each other and the whole.

  [4.RL.5] [5.RL.5] [6.RL.5] [7.RL.5] [8.RL.5]

- **Demonstrate** understanding of figurative language, word relationships, and nuances in word meanings.

  [4.L.5] [5.L.5] [6.L.5] [7.L.5] [8.L.5]

- **Interpret** words and phrases as they are used in a text, including determining technical, connotative, and figurative meanings, and analyze how specific word choices shape meaning or tone.

  [4.RIT.4] [5.RIT.4] [6.RIT.4] [7.RIT.4] [8.RIT.4]

- **Write** informative/explanatory texts to examine and convey complex ideas and information clearly and accurately through the effective selection, organization, and analysis of content.

  [4.W.2] [5.W.2] [6.W.2] [7.W.2] [8.W.2]

- **Write** narrative to develop real or imagined experiences or events using effective technique, well-chosen details, and well-structured sequences.

  [4.W.3] [5.W.3] [6.W.3] [7.W.3] [8.W.3]

- **Produce** clear and coherent writing in which the development, organization, and style are appropriate to task, purpose, and audience.

  [4.W.4] [5.W.4] [6.W.4] [7.W.4] [8.W.4]

- **Use** knowledge of language conventions.

  [4.L.3] [5.L.3] [6.L.3] [7.L.3] [8.L.3]

PRIOR TO THE LESSON

- Read through entire lesson and review the slideshow to familiarize yourself with the clinic.

- Note that one of the bonus poems at the end of this clinic may be better suited to use as a model for your class than the one embedded in the clinic. Select the poem that works best for you and your students—your choice.

- Set up a separate surface (chart paper or white board) on which to compose a poem written collectively by you and your students.

- Consider having a list of prepositions handy. (We've included one in the slides.)

- Note that this lesson works best if the students have previously been introduced to prepositions.

THE LESSON

Slide 1

- Introduce the teaching poets by name (Sara and Michael), as they will appear throughout this lesson.

Slides 2–3

- Explain to students that they are going to build a better understanding of prepositional phrases and how to put them to good use in writing.
- Explain that we are going to climb up and over, across and through in order to write a prepositional poem.

Slide 4

- Review what a prepositional phrase is.

Slide 5

- Read or have students read these phrases aloud.
- Ask if students can think of others. (See next slide for some ideas.)

Slide 6

- Use this list to help students think of things a monkey could do to a mountain.
- Add a prepositional phrase to a complete sentence to describe movement and setting.

Slide 7

- Help students avoid clichés with this list.
- Mix and match from either column. Encourage creative pairings, such as *over the television, after the bell, through the bus.*
- Note that although these may not end up in the writers' pieces, the exercise will open them up to be more creative while remaining true to the structure.

Slide 8

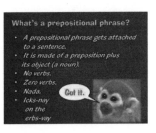

- Reinforce the difference between a complete sentence, a clause, and a phrase.
- Remind students that the prepositional phrase can modify a noun or a verb.

Text Talk

Slide 9

- Point out that the poem "Love Heals" contains prepositional phrases mixed in with some complete sentences to form a pattern.

Slides 10–12: "Love Heals" by Sara Holbrook

- Read the poem aloud, have a different student read each verse (three verses), and/or play the audio (on Slide 13).
- See Slide 12 or 13 to examine the poem all on one page.

Slide 13

- Have students turn and talk about the meaning of the poem.
- Ask: How does love heal? (Smiles, healing a fractured spirit.)
- Ask: Can you make any personal connections to this poem?
- Note the pattern of the poem—three prepositional phrases modifying three simple sentences.
- Point out that if you break this poem down, the three sentences could stand alone. (We share smiles / I stumble / She pours glue.)
- Reiterate that a prepositional phrase modifies a noun or a verb.
- Define *modify* for the students: to modify is to change.
- Ask: What do the prepositional phrases add to this poem? (Visual language that adds setting and motion to the poem.)

Slide 14: "Five-Paragraph Essay" by Michael Salinger

- Read the poem aloud, have a student read it, and/or play the audio.
- Ask: Have you ever been there on a Sunday night?
- Ask: Structurally, how is this poem different from the preceding one, "Love Heals"? (This poem has only one sentence in it; "Love Heals" has three.)

- Note: Writing a prepositional poem requires at least one anchor sentence, but the poem may include more than one sentence.

- Note: The prepositional phrases modify (change) the sentences by adding important details about the setting of the poem.

Work Together

Slide 15

- Explain that we will work together as a class to compose a prepositional poem about this picture.

- Have students partner up and get out their writer's notebooks, laptops, tablets, or a piece of paper.

- Write the sentence "The boy walks" in the middle of your writing surface.

- Ask: What prepositional phrases could be added to modify the sentence "The boy walks"?

- Ask each pair of writers to come up with at least three prepositional phrases to modify this simple sentence.

- Give students about 3 minutes to come up with them.

- Ask students to volunteer phrases and add them above and below the sentence "The boy walks." (Responses will sound something like this: *along the street, beside the grass, through the sunshine.*)

- Ask students if they would like to add another sentence or rearrange lines to craft the poem.

- Don't spend too much time doing this (no more than 5 minutes), as you are just modeling the system students will use to write their poems.

Slide 16

- Ask students to open their writer's notebooks, laptops, or tablets, or take out a piece of paper.

- Ask them to choose an image to write about. (See slide for some ideas.)

- Consider asking students to choose an image focused around a unit of study. Alternatively, have them select an image from their memory or imagination.

- Challenge students to use as least three to five prepositional phrases in their poems.

- Ask students to begin by composing a simple sentence about the image.

- Tell students this sentence may not even turn up in the final poem, but that it is a place to start.

- Leave the poem you wrote as a class visible so students can refer to the model.

Slide 17

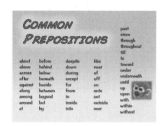

- Instruct students to refer to this list as it might help them in their writing process.
- Circulate around as students are writing.
- Note, it is not uncommon for writers to need a reminder about how a prepositional phrase works.
- Remind them of the monkey and the mountain.

Time to Revise

Slide 18

- Remind students that we are not just randomly listing prepositional phrases.
- Emphasize that we are using prepositional phrases to modify nouns and verbs in order to modify our images.
- Ask students to first revise by reading aloud to everyone at the same time. Seat symphony!
- Ask students to read to a partner and give one another feedback on their poem drafts.

Share

Slide 19

- Ask students to take turns sharing aloud.

Slide 20

- Remind students that a prepositional phrase modifies (changes) a verb or a noun, making it more descriptive.
- Note that using prepositional phrases can add imagery to our writing.
- Tell students that prepositional phrases also add setting and motion.

Bonus Poems and Lesson Extensions

Slide 21

- These bonus poems have been selected to give you the opportunity to differentiate according to the needs of your classroom and to extend and reinforce the lesson.

Slide 22: "About My MVP Award" by Allan Wolf

- Read the poem aloud, have a student read it, and/or play the audio.

- Ask: What is the setting of this poem? (A soccer field.)

- Ask: What do the prepositional phrases do for this poem? (They show movement as the player is moving the ball down the field.)

- Provide students with background information about the poet:

  - Across the page and around the world, Allan Wolf is an award-winning poet/performer. A delightful, insightful writer and presenter, he hails from North Carolina. You can get to know him better by visiting his website: www.allanwolf.com.

Slide 23: "Spring and All" by William Carlos Williams

- Notice how in this poem William Carlos Williams begins by setting a scene using prepositional phrases.

- Click on the button to read the poem.

- Consider that younger students may want to analyze only the first verse. Invite older students to analyze the entire poem.

- Ask students to identify the prepositional phrases.

- Ask: What do the modifying phrases add to the poem?

- Provide students with background information about the poet:

  - Most students are introduced to William Carlos Williams with his poem "The Red Wheelbarrow." Williams, a poet and a physician, was part of what was called the Imagist movement. He then went on to experiment, creating strong images that capture a moment in time. You can find out more about Williams at www.poets.org/poet.php/prmPID/119.

ASSESSMENT

Here we provide a rubric you may choose to use. We provide this as a guide knowing that you may have other goals for your class. Don't feel compelled to assess every skill mentioned in this chart. We have had more success when we zero in on a skill or two with a lesson, but we want to afford you multiple options with these clinics.

Skill	3	2	1
Careful Reading	Demonstrates an understanding of how the use of setting in a piece adds to the tone. Recognizes prepositional phrases in text and understands their role in modifying nouns and verbs.	Partially demonstrates an understanding of how the use of setting in a piece adds to the overall tone. Occasionally confuses a phrase with a clause or misidentifies what is being modified by a prepositional phrase.	Does not demonstrate an understanding of how the use of setting in a piece adds to the overall tone. Cannot distinguish between a phrase and a clause. Cannot identify prepositions or explain what they modify.
Structure and Organization	Demonstrates the ability to recognize and re-create a writing structure, utilizing prepositional phrases as a means to establish setting and motion. Avoids cliché.	Partially demonstrates the ability to recognize and re-create writing structures, utilizing prepositional phrases as a means to establish setting and motion. Occasionally may lapse into cliché.	Does not demonstrate the ability to compose a simple sentence with a modifying phrase. May create prepositional phrases that modify nothing.
Grammar Conventions	Demonstrates an understanding of the terms *noun, verb, simple sentence,* and *modifying phrase.*	Partially demonstrates an understanding of the terms *noun, verb, simple sentence,* and *modifying phrase.* May occasionally misidentify these terms.	Does not demonstrate an understanding of the terms *noun, verb, simple sentence,* and *modifying phrase.* Misidentifies the majority of these terms.
Speaking Skills	Consistently demonstrates effective presentation skills using good voice projection, inflection, pacing, eye contact, and stance.	Partially demonstrates effective presentation skills using good voice projection, inflection, pacing, eye contact, and stance.	Does not demonstrate effective presentation skills using good voice projection, inflection, pacing, eye contact, and stance.
Listening Skills	Actively participates in discussions about other students' work and is tuned in to student presentations.	Occasionally participates in discussions about other students' work and is tuned in to student presentations.	Does not participate in discussions about other students' work and is not tuned in to student presentations.

15

Simile for Me

WHY TEACH THIS?

It was just like . . .

Just like what?

Comparisons are *like* the backbone of figurative language—they are as essential to creating meaning as syrup is to pancakes. Similes show how two things that are not alike in most ways are similar in one *important* way. Similes work because they ask our readers to imagine the comparison, to weigh its validity against their own experience, and to stop and think a bit.

This writing clinic is designed to give your students practice with using similes in their own writing. We will discuss the difference between a simile and a metaphor, share some examples of similes in action, and then try our hands at writing some ourselves.

Sara: With a simile, I take an experience of mine and explain that it is like something you already know about. I want you to get what I'm talking about.

Michael: Well, that's as clear as mud.

Sara: I see what you did there.

CCSS AND CORRESPONDING ANCHOR STANDARDS

- **Demonstrate** understanding of figurative language, word relationships, and nuances in word meanings.

  [4.L.5] [5.L.5] [6.L.5] [7.L.5] [8.L.5]

- **Determine** the meaning of words and phrases as they are used in text, including technical, connotative, and figurative meanings, and analyze how specific word choices shape meaning or tone.

  [4.RIT.4] [5.RIT.4] [6.RIT.4] [7.RIT.4] [8.RIT.4]

- **Determine** the meaning of words and phrases as they are used in a text, including figurative and cognitive meanings; analyze the impact of a specific word choice on meaning and tone.

  [4.RL.4] [5.RL.4] [6.RL.4] [7.RL.4] [8.RL.4]

- **Read** and comprehend complex literary and informational texts independently and proficiently.

  [4.RL.10] [5.RL.10] [6.RL.10] [7.RL.10] [8.RL.10]

- **Produce** clear and coherent writing in which the development, organization, and style are appropriate to task, purpose, and audience.

  [4.W.4] [5.W.4] [6.W.4] [7.W.4] [8.W.4]

PRIOR TO THE LESSON

- Read through the entire lesson and review the slideshow to familiarize yourself with the clinic.

- Note that one of the bonus poems at the end of this clinic may be better suited to use as a model for your class than the one embedded in the clinic. Select the poem that works best for you and your students—your choice.

- Set up a separate surface (chart paper or white board) on which to compose a poem written collectively by you and your students.

THE LESSON

Slide 1

- Introduce the teaching poets by name (Sara and Michael), as they will appear throughout this lesson.

Slide 2

- Explain to students that we are going to examine a poem that uses similes.

- Tell students that we are then going to write an amazing poem using similes.

Slide 3

- Discuss with your class what a simile is.

- Explain to students that a simile is a comparison of two different things using the words *like, as, if,* and *than*.

Text Talk

Slides 4–8

- Read the poem aloud, have a student read it, and/or play the audio (on Slide 9).

- Continue through Slides 5, 6, 7, and 8.

Slide 9

- Here is the entire poem.
- Identify the similes in this poem.
- Discuss how the similes zero in on one specific detail in the comparison.
- Explain that this specificity makes for a stronger comparison. Rather than saying something is like Cleveland, Ohio, for instance, Sara says something is as rusty as Cleveland.
- Note that this specific comparison steers the interpretation of the figurative language.

Work Together

Slide 10

- Prepare to write a poem together.
- Consider using this image of a clown as a writing prompt, but you may wish to choose an image from your content area of study (*a fraction is me, a proton is me, the scientific process is me*).
- Write the LAST line of the poem FIRST at the bottom of your workspace. In this case it would be *A clown is me*.
- Prompt students to think about specific parts of the clown image: the shape of the clown's hat, the sounds he may make, the color of his shirt and nose, his face paint, his wide open eyes.
- Ask students to come up with suggestions for similes from the point of view of the clown.
- Encourage suggestions that sound like this:
  - Eyes as big as bicycle wheels
  - Nose redder than an apple
  - Hat shaped like a chocolate kiss
- Choose four or five of these suggestions and write them on the board above the last line.
- Use this as your simile poem, Version 1.

Time to Write

Slide 11

- Ask students to get out their writer's notebooks, paper, computer, or tablet.
- Prompt them to pick a topic they are passionate about.
- See the slide for some examples.
- Have students turn and talk with a partner about what their last line will be before they begin to write.

- Circulate around the room and make sure everyone has identified a topic and knows what his or her last line will be.
- Remind students that they can write from their own point of view or an alternative point of view, such as the point of view of the pencil the boy is holding in the picture.
- Give them 2–3 minutes to identify their topic.
- Instruct them to write their last line first just as we did in the model.
- Give students 10 minutes to compose their Version 1 drafts.

Share

Slide 12

- Ask students to first read their drafts aloud, everyone reading at the same time. Seat symphony!
- Invite students to share with a partner.
- Have fun with the reading: Go around the room and have students read their favorite simile that they have created.
- Ask for enthusiastic volunteers to read to the class.
- Reinforce powerful similes when you hear them.

Slide 13

- Explain that similes engage readers through comparisons that bring our writing to life.
- Emphasize that the more specific the comparison, the stronger it is.
- Use Michael's example: *Crazy as a bug* versus *Crazy as a bug drinking gasoline*.

Bonus Poems and Lesson Extensions

Slide 14

- These bonus poems have been selected to give you the opportunity to differentiate according to the needs of your classroom and to extend and reinforce the lesson.

Slide 15: "Flint" by Christina Rossetti

- Give students some basic background: This is a poem using simile by Christina Rossetti, first published in 1872.
- Read the poem aloud, have a student read it, and/or play the audio.

- Ask students to identify the similes.
- Provide students with some background information about the author:
  - Christina Rossetti was born and raised in London; however, her parents were Italian. She was quite famous in her time. You can find out more information about her at www.poetryfoundation.org/bio/christina-rossetti.

Slide 16: "Like Me or Knot" by Nikki Grimes

- Read the poem aloud, have a student read it, and/or play the audio.
- Notice how this poem teases the reader by not exactly naming what the poet is talking about.
- Ask: What might we scrunch, tie, or let fly free? (See next slide.)

Slide 17

- A scarf!
- Note that students may want to write their own mystery poems, naming some similes that lead the reader to the answer.
- Provide students with some background information about the poet:
  - Nikki Grimes is an award-winning poet and author and a winner of the National Council of Teachers of English Excellence in Children's Poetry Award. She lives in California and is also a talented artist and photographer. You can find more information about her at www.nikkigrimes.com.

Slide 18: "The Longest Home Run" by J. Patrick Lewis

- Read the poem aloud, have a student read it, and/or play the audio.
- Point out that in this simile poem, the poet does not even use the word *like*; instead he uses the word *than*.
- Ask students to find the comparisons.
- Consider having students write their own measurement simile poems. What about? Discuss!
- Provide students with some background information about the poet:
  - J. Patrick Lewis is a former U.S. Children's Poet Laureate and a winner of the National Council of Teachers of English Excellence in Children's Poetry Award. His books are both fun and chock full of all kinds of information. Please check out his website: http://jpatricklewis.com.

Slide 19: "A Poem Is . . ." by Michael Salinger

- Read the poem aloud, have a student read it, and/or play the audio.
- Ask: What details does Michael use to build his similes? (He doesn't stop with just comparing poetry to Kool-Aid; he says it is like Kool-Aid with the *water gone*—not just eyeglasses, but eyeglasses for *nose and ears*.)

ASSESSMENT

Here we provide a rubric you may choose to use. We provide this as a guide knowing that you may have other goals for your class. Don't feel compelled to assess every skill mentioned in this chart. We have had more success when we zero in on a skill or two with a lesson, but we want to afford you multiple options with these clinics.

Skill	3	2	1
Careful Reading	Demonstrates an understanding of the importance of using comparisons to clarify writing. Knows the difference between simile and metaphor. Is able to articulate meaning beyond the literal.	Partially demonstrates an understanding of the importance of using comparisons to clarify writing. May occasionally misidentify similes as comparisons other than those that use the word *like*.	Does not demonstrate an understanding of the importance of using comparisons to clarify writing. Cannot recognize simile in text.
Structure and Organization	Demonstrates the ability to recognize and re-create a writing structure that includes simile comparisons. Similes created are insightful, nuanced, and contain strong detail.	Partially demonstrates the ability to recognize and re-create a writing structure that includes simile comparisons. Some similes may be cliché or lack supporting detail.	Does not demonstrate the ability to recognize and re-create a writing structure that includes simile comparisons. Assessed work contains no similes.
Connotative Word Meaning	Demonstrates an understanding of connotative word meanings by making comparisons while using visual language. Uses simile creatively and effectively.	Occasionally demonstrates an understanding of connotative word meanings by making comparisons while using visual language. Similes don't necessarily clarify the meaning of the piece and/or may be cliché.	Does not demonstrate an understanding of connotative word meanings by making comparisons while using visual language. Writing is void of simile.
Speaking Skills	Consistently demonstrates effective presentation skills using good voice projection, inflection, pacing, eye contact, and stance.	Partially demonstrates effective presentation skills using good voice projection, inflection, pacing, eye contact, and stance.	Does not demonstrate effective presentation skills using good voice projection, inflection, pacing, eye contact, and stance.
Listening Skills	Actively participates in discussions about other students' work and is tuned in to student presentations.	Occasionally participates in discussions about other students' work and is tuned in to student presentations.	Does not participate in discussions about other students' work and is not tuned in to student presentations.

16

Metaphor Mentor Text

WHY TEACH THIS?

We're a pair of grumpy bears before we have our morning coffee.

Okay, you know we are not literally foul-smelling hirsute members of the Ursus genus each morning who only assume human form after a cup of coffee. This description is a metaphor—a comparison used to help our audience understand that we may not be suitable for polite company until we get a bit of early morning caffeine into our systems.

Metaphor is a tricky bit of figurative language that requires us to think more deeply than we ordinarily do when we're considering the literal meaning of words. Not only does metaphor require us to hold, compare, contrast, and judge a couple of possibly very disparate images in our minds, but it invites us to do so in a way that is somewhat subjective.

This writing clinic is designed to help your students understand and write metaphors with the aid of mentor texts, and it is the first in our suite of three metaphor-related clinics. Just like a drawing student may go to the local museum to find exemplary pieces of art from which to draw inspiration and begin a sketch, we want to give our writing students examples to follow so that they can become comfortable with this communication device.

Sara: This is a higher-order thinking skill. In this clinic, we are helping students take their initial steps toward understanding and subsequently using metaphor.

Michael: Sara, you're a peach!

CCSS AND CORRESPONDING ANCHOR STANDARDS

- **Demonstrate** command of the conventions of standard English grammar and usage when writing or speaking.

  [4.L.1] [5.L.1] [6.L.1] [7.L.1] [8.L.1]

- **Demonstrate** understanding of figurative language, word relationships, and nuances in word meanings.

  [4.L.5] [5.L.5] [6.L.5] [7.L.5] [8.L.5]

- **Interpret** words and phrases as they are used in a text, including determining technical, connotative, and figurative meanings, and analyze how specific word choices shape meaning or tone.

  [4.RL.4] [5.RL.4] [6.RL.4] [7.RL.4] [8.RL.4]

- **Analyze** the structure of texts, including how specific sentences, paragraphs, and larger portions of the text (e.g., a section, chapter, scene, or stanza) relate to each other and the whole.

  [4.RL.5] [5.RL.5] [6.RL.5] [7.RL.5] [8.RL.5]

- **Read** and comprehend complex literary and informational texts independently and proficiently.

  [4.RL.10] [5.RL.10] [6.RL.10] [7.RL.10] [8.RL.10]

- **Write** informative/explanatory texts to examine and convey complex ideas and information clearly and accurately through the effective selection, organization, and analysis of content.

  [4.W.2] [5.W.2] [6.W.2] [7.W.2] [8.W.2]

- **Produce** clear and coherent writing in which the development, organization, and style are appropriate to task, purpose, and audience.

  [4.W.4] [5.W.4] [6.W.4] [7.W.4] [8.W.4]

PRIOR TO THE LESSON

- Read through entire lesson and review slideshow to familiarize yourself with the clinic.

- Note that one of the bonus poems at the end of this clinic may be better suited to use as a model for your class than the one embedded in the clinic. Select the poem that works best for you and your students—your choice.

- Set up a separate surface (chart paper or white board) on which to compose a poem written collectively by you and your students.

- This clinic is presented in two parts; you may decide to take two class sessions to complete both.

- Consider completing the simile clinic prior to this clinic.

THE LESSON

Slide 1

- Introduce teaching poets by name (Michael and Sara), as they will appear throughout this lesson.

Slide 2

- Look to the far right in this slide. There is a monitor lizard poking his head into the shot.

- Like a metaphor, he isn't too obvious.

Slide 3

- Backstory: This monitor lizard was about 4 feet long, had a menacing tail, and could almost make himself invisible. Sara and Michael encountered him at the Botanical Garden in Singapore.

- Explain that, using this description, we decided he was a metaphor for a metaphor.

Slide 4

- Note that this lesson has two parts and two writing assignments.

- Decide whether you would like to split the lesson into 2 days.

- Remember, sifting through poetry to find metaphors can be tedious work.

- Building metaphors, on the other hand, can be fun and will help raise students' awareness of metaphor as they study the craft of other writers.

Slide 5

- Here is a simple definition of *metaphor*.

- Emphasize that the important part of this definition is that a metaphor is a comparison.

- Ask: Why do we make comparisons? (To determine what is the same or different between things, to define ideas via common images.)

Slide 6

- Read these two examples aloud:
  - The child's face was like a blossom ready to burst into to bloom = simile.
  - The child's face, a blossom ready to burst into bloom = metaphor.

- Note that we speak in metaphor all the time. (That truck is a monster. She is a ray of sunshine. He is a bolt of lightning.)

- Have students turn and talk to come up with other examples.

- Ask students to offer their ideas to the class.

- Correct misperceptions.

Slide 7

- Join the conversation (next three slides).

- Get kids involved by having them read the thought bubbles aloud.
  - Sometimes metaphors are mysterious.
  - A metaphor is a monitor lizard hiding in the bushes?

Slide 8

- A flower about to bloom?

Slide 9

- Nuts in my chocolate cream?
- This is a clue to the next poem.

Text Talk

Slides 10–12

- Read the poem with your students.
- This is going to be the mentor text for students.

Work Together

Slide 13: "Disappointment" by Sara Holbrook

- Remember, this is going to be the mentor text for your group write.
- Announce that you will change the title of the poem to an emotion (Excitement? Terror? Amazement?), a place (home, school, orchestra, or band), or an event (basketball game, war, swim meet). You choose.
- Write the chosen topic on a separate surface, white board, or chart paper.
- Note: For the purposes of our Version 1 draft, let's start with *What a surprise*, which indicates a "wow" moment.

Slide 14

- Read this first sample, "Terror," and note how it follows the pattern of the mentor text. Three lines read something like this:
  - You're spiders crawling in my brain.
  - You're a face in the window.
  - You're chains dragging across the floor.
- Note: We are not looking for simple actions, as in *Terror, you shivered*. We are looking for something more like *Terror, you are leaves on a windy day.*
- Ask: Can you think of some other lines that might fit with these metaphors for *terror*?
- Correct misperceptions.

Slide 15

- Read the second sample "Fractions."

- Remember: For the purposes of our Version 1 draft, we are starting with *What a surprise,* which indicates a "wow" moment.

- Ask students to turn and talk about possibilities for a group write, using the pattern of the mentor text.

- Decide on a topic and write it on the board or chart paper.

- Ask students to contribute three or four lines.

- Write these on the board.

- Do not spend too much time on this; you are simply modeling the process.

- Leave your group poem visible as a model as the students do their own writing, or flip back to Slide 13.

Time to Write

Slide 16

- Ask students to get out their writer's notebooks, paper, computers, or tablets.

- Announce that students may work alone or in pairs.

- Ask the students to choose a topic and write it down at the top of their papers/documents.

- Begin the writing process with a discussion. Regardless of whether students ultimately choose to write solo or if they are writing with a partner, ask them to confer before writing.

- Ask students to talk over some comparisons to use for metaphors, offering ideas and sharing creative thoughts.

- Give them about 2 minutes for discussion, then announce it is time to begin writing.

- Allot 12–15 minutes for a first draft.

- Say NO! when the first person asks if the poem has to rhyme.

- Say YES! when the first person asks if it is okay to rhyme. (But the poem has to be logical. Rhyme is never enough.)

Share

Slide 17

- Begin by having students read their drafts aloud at the same time. Seat symphony!

- Invite students to share with a partner.

- Have a few students share with the class.

- Extend this exercise by asking students to publish their poems as a short movie or PowerPoint, choosing images that reflect the comparisons. An old-fashioned poster would also work. This is a fun poem to illustrate.

Part 2: The Topography of Me

Slide 18

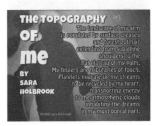

- Ask: What landscape items do you see in this picture? (Mountains, a lake or pond, foothills, grass, scrub brush, rocks, etc.)

Text Talk

Slide 19: "Topography of Me" by Sara Holbrook

- Read the mentor text aloud, have a student read it, and/or play the audio.
- Ask one half of the class to collaborate to find the topography terms in the mentor text (*landscape, populated, forests, plateau,* etc.).
- Ask the other half of the class to identify the human parts of the poem. (There aren't as many: *arm, shoulders, palm, fingers, platelets, heart.*)

Work Together

Slide 20

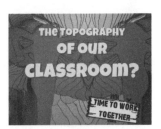

- Announce that you are going to work together on a poem using *topography* terms to describe the classroom (see the next slide).

Slide 21

- Note: Metaphor happens when we use words describing one thing to describe another.
- Ask students to look over these terms and research words for which they do not know the meaning.
- Ask something like: Is there a stream in this classroom? Which of these words do you see in the landscape of this classroom?
- Have students turn and talk over ideas.
- Write down suggestions as they come up. (They will sound like this: The inhabitants of this classroom migrate into the room each day to fill the atmosphere with learning—or some such observation.)

Time to Write

- Ask: What is the topography of the lunch room? Of the football or soccer field? Of yourself or your family?
- Note that this is only a partial list of geographic terms, with a little research the students will find more.

Slide 22

- Suggest other lists of terms students might use to build metaphors, such as digestive terms.
- Ask if students can think of others. (Parts of a skeleton, parts of an essay, parts of a car.)

Share

Slide 23

- Ask students to share their poems with a partner.
- Invite a few students to share with the class.

Slide 24

- Reiterate that we can communicate our ideas more effectively when we use comparisons in our writing.

Bonus Poems and Lesson Extensions

Slide 25

- These bonus poems have been selected to give you the opportunity to differentiate according to the needs of your classroom and to extend and reinforce the lesson.

Slide 26: "Divided" by Sara Holbrook

- Read the poem aloud, have a student read it, and/or play the audio.
- Ask: What is the poet talking about? (Divorce.)
- Ask: Can you find the math terms in this poem? (*Unit, divided, add, subtract, multiply.*)

Slide 27: "He Had His Dream" by Paul Laurence Dunbar

- Familiarize students with the words *bark, tempest,* and *tincture.*
- Provide some historical background information on the poet.
  - Dunbar (1872–1906) grew up in Dayton, Ohio. He was a classmate of the Wright Brothers. He was the author of 12 books of poetry and many short stories and plays. He was the first African American poet to come to prominence before dying of tuberculosis at the age of 33. For more information, visit www.dunbarsite.org.

Slide 28

- Read the poem aloud, play the audio, or visit the Paul Laurence Dunbar website to hear an actor read the poem: www.dunbarsite.org/gallery/HeHadHisDream .asp. (After following the link, click on the high-speed connection option.)

- Ask: Is this really a poem about a man just sailing in a boat? (It could mean a person traveling through life.)

- Ask: What might be some examples of "storms" in life? (Challenges such as prejudice, poverty, death of a loved one, etc.)

- Ask: How did the poet use his metaphor to communicate his ideas? (He gave us an image of a man steering a boat to represent a person going through life.)

- Remember that Dunbar wrote and published a generation before Langston Hughes. For further reading have students research "Dreams" and "A Dream Deferred" by Langston Hughes (readily available on the Internet).

Slide 29: "Blessing the Boats" by Lucille Clifton

- Note that Lucille Clifton wrote this little poem to bless the ships at St. Mary's.

- Click on the blue button above and read the poem or have a student read it.

- Note: Every religion and culture we can think of has its own versions of "blessings."

- Ask: What is a blessing? (A prayer asking for safety, or in this case, smooth sailing.)

- Consider this as a writing prompt for students: Using Clifton's poem as a guide, write a blessing for something in your own life. (A blessing for a school bus, a new pair of sneakers or jeans, the sun—entertain some ideas from students.)

- Click on the brown button to hear Clifton read her poem "Won't You Celebrate With Me."

- Note: This is the only poet we have linked to two separate poems. We have no excuse for this except we just couldn't help ourselves.

- Enjoy!

- Ask students to listen to Clifton, then compare her poem to Dunbar's (Slide 28). Do they have similar themes?

- Provide students with some background information about the poet:

  ○ Lucille Clifton moves her readers through direct language and real-world situations. Her honors include an Emmy Award from the American Academy of Television Arts and Sciences, a Lannan Literary Award, two fellowships from the National Endowment for the Arts, the Shelley Memorial Award, the YM-YWHA Poetry Center Discovery Award, and the Ruth Lilly Prize, in addition to two of her books being nominated for Pulitzer Prizes. If you are not acquainted with her, find out more at www.poets.org/poet.php/prmPID/79.

Slide 30: "Belay Off" by Michael Salinger

- Prior to reading the poem, ask if anyone in the class has experience with rock climbing. (Many kids have tried climbing on rock walls.)

- Ask: What does it mean to "Belay Off"? (It means when you unhook yourself from the safety line.)

- Familiarize students with these two words before reading the poem: A *carabineer* is a clip and *cams* are what you shove in the rocks so that you can grab hold.

- Before reading, ask students to listen to the poem to see if they can make a personal connection. The connection could be about climbing a mountain, falling, or looking down from a high altitude, just as long as they find any line they can connect with.

- Read the poem aloud, have a student read it, and/or play the audio (on the next slide).

Slide 31

- Invite a few students to articulate their personal connections to the poem after reading it aloud to the class.

- Note: Often poets bury a metaphor in a poem, expecting that you will take the poet's experience and compare it to one of your own.

- Ask: Besides rock climbing, what could the poet be talking about when he refers to surmounting an obstacle? (Obstacles include all of life's challenges.)

- Ask: What else could the poet mean by "they tell you to never look down"? (Climbing any obstacle requires some risks. Don't freak out!)

- Ask: Does the poet ever say, "Rock climbing is like life." (No. He relates his experience and lets the reader drawn his or her own conclusions.)

ASSESSMENT

Here we provide a rubric you may choose to use. We provide this as a guide knowing that you may have other goals for your class. Don't feel compelled to assess every skill mentioned in this chart. We have had more success when we zero in on a skill or two with a lesson, but we want to afford you multiple options with these clinics.

Skill	3	2	1
Careful Reading	Demonstrates an understanding of the importance of using comparisons to clarify our writing. Knows the difference between simile and metaphor. Is able to articulate meaning beyond the literal.	Partially demonstrates an understanding of the importance of using comparisons to clarify our writing. May mistakenly interpret some metaphors literally.	Does not demonstrate an understanding of the importance of using comparisons to clarify our writing. Cannot recognize metaphor in text.
Structure and Organization	Demonstrates the ability to recognize and re-create a writing structure that includes metaphorical comparisons. Creates metaphors that are insightful and nuanced.	Partially demonstrates the ability to recognize and re-create a writing structure that includes metaphorical comparisons. May create some metaphors that are cliché or illogical.	Does not demonstrate the ability to recognize and re-create a writing structure that includes metaphorical comparisons. Cannot move beyond literal meaning.
Connotative Word Meaning	Demonstrates an understanding of connotative word meanings by making comparisons while using visual language. Metaphors are used creatively and effectively.	Occasionally demonstrates an understanding of connotative word meanings by making comparisons while using visual language. Metaphors don't necessarily clarify the meaning of the piece.	Does not demonstrate an understanding of connotative word meanings by making comparisons while using visual language. Writing is void of metaphor.
Speaking Skills	Consistently demonstrates effective presentation skills using good voice projection, inflection, pacing, eye contact, and stance.	Partially demonstrates effective presentation skills using good voice projection, inflection, pacing, eye contact, and stance.	Does not demonstrate effective presentation skills using good voice projection, inflection, pacing, eye contact, and stance.
Listening Skills	Actively participates in discussions about other students' work and is tuned in to student presentations.	Occasionally participates in discussions about other students' work and is tuned in to student presentations.	Does not participate in discussions about other students' work and is not tuned in to student presentations.

17

Exquisite Metaphors

Comparing Apples and Oranges

WHY TEACH THIS?

Exquisite Corpse is a turn-of-the-20th-century parlor game that we use to help teach analysis of metaphor. To play the game, we create a sentence from random words that are chosen according to their parts of speech so that when they are assembled into a sentence, they are grammatically correct, but not necessarily logical. This will make more sense once we get into the clinic. We like it because the sentences created by this game are—by design—a little bit cryptic. It's this fuzziness that leads our students to think more deeply when they assign meaning to the sentences that are created by the game.

If your classroom has been stricken with weaker-than-a-kitten clichéd comparisons, hook them up to this creativity infusion. Let their imaginations loose as they try to decide if that toaster in the basement is lonely or apprehensive. Here, students will be challenged to assign meaning to seemingly meaningless phrases and then support their analysis with explanatory text in the form of a poem. This clinic is designed to get kids to stretch common words into uncommon comparisons in order to create strong metaphors that are unique.

Michael: This is one of my favorites because it forces the writers to find meaning through reader response—something I think might get lost in our multiple-choice test-taking paradigms.

Sara: Personally, I tend to be rooted in reality—maybe a little too much. So this is a clinic I feel has benefitted me personally as it affords me permission to trek across unfamiliar paths.

CCSS AND CORRESPONDING ANCHOR STANDARDS

- **Demonstrate** understanding of figurative language, word relationships, and nuances in word meanings.

  [4.L.5] [5.L.5] [6.L.5] [7.L.5] [8.L.5]

- **Determine** the meaning of words and phrases as they are used in text, including technical, connotative, and figurative meanings and analyze how specific word choices shape meaning or tone.

  [4.RIT.4] [5.RIT.4] [6.RIT.4] [7.RIT.4] [8.RIT.4]

- **Determine** the meaning of words and phrases as they are used in a text, including figurative and cognitive meanings; analyze the impact of a specific word choice on meaning and tone.

  [4.RL.4] [5.RL.4] [6.RL.4] [7.RL.4] [8.RL.4]

- **Produce** clear and coherent writing in which the development, organization, and style are appropriate to task, purpose, and audience.

  [4.W.4] [5.W.4] [6.W.4] [7.W.4] [8.W.4]

PRIOR TO THE LESSON

- Read through the entire lesson and review the slideshow to familiarize yourself with the clinic.

- Each student will need six slips of paper (torn-up recycled paper, index cards, sticky notes, etc.).

- Note that one of the bonus poems at the end of this clinic may be better suited to use as a model for your class than the one embedded in the clinic. Select the poem that works best for you and your students—your choice.

- Set up a separate surface (chart paper or white board) on which to compose a poem written collectively by you and your students.

- Consider preceding this lesson with Clinic 14: Prepositional Phrase Poem and Clinic 16: Metaphor Mentor Text.

THE LESSON

Slide 1

- Introduce the teaching poets by name (Sara and Michael), as they will appear throughout this lesson.

Slide 2

- Ask: What are we going to learn today?

- Explain: We are going to read about and use figurative language.

- Say: We are going to look at a frightened blue toaster dancing in the basement and see what we can make of that.

Slide 3

- Define figurative language as using a word or phrase to represent something other than what it is, that is, something other than its literal meaning.

- Use the phrases on this slide as an example. Neither of the dogs pictured are vehicles that can carry passengers, although the mastiff comes close.

- Ask students to turn and talk about other examples. (*This car is a moose. She is a mouse. His heart is a stone.*)

Slide 4

- Ask: How can words be like automatic weapons?

- Ask: Why do you think that the poet used this comparison? See the full text of this poem in the bonus poem section at the end of the clinic.

Slide 5

- Ask: What is a piston? Where are some places pistons can be found? (Also found in a car engine.)

- Ask: What do pistons do to an engine?

- Ask: Why would the poet compare the cyclist's legs to locomotive pistons? (Locomotives are more powerful than, say, a car.)

- See the full text of this poem in the bonus poem section at the end of the clinic.

Slide 6

- Reminder: Interpreting poetry is never a sure thing.

- Explain that, without actually asking the poet, "What did you mean by that?" the reader is left to guess or infer what the poet means.

- Let students know that this guessing requires us to draw on our own experience in order to create meaning when we encounter new and creative connections.

- Clarify that while technically there is no wrong way to interpret figurative language, we still need a logical rationale for our interpretations.

- Describe how we come to a consensus meaning for a piece of writing— when the same interpretation appears over and over for a piece of creative writing, this interpretation may become the accepted meaning.

- Be careful about rejecting a novel interpretation until listening to the reasoning behind it.

- Remember, one of our goals is to encourage deeper reading and creative thinking.

Slide 7

- Use this as another opportunity to discuss clichés.

- Explain: Some comparisons, while unique the first time they were used, have become so common that we call them cliché. (*Deer in the headlights, nails on a chalkboard.*)

- Explain: Here are two easy ways to recognize a cliché:
  - Begin the phrase and if listeners can finish the phrase, chances are good it is a cliché.
  - Type the phrase into Google. If Google is able to finish the phrase, you've most likely got a cliché on your hands.
- Note that this clinic is designed to help the students make comparisons that are unique.

Slide 8

- Say: It is raining hats.
- Point out that this is an absurd statement.
- Expand on this for students. It is a sentence, but the sentence still stretches logic, even with an illustration.

Slide 9

- Show students that by adding to this statement, we can see this sentence as a play on words.
- Ask: What is the well-known expression we are playing with? (It is raining cats and dogs.)
- Word play is fun!

Slide 10

- Describe: Before there were family rooms, video games, and karaoke, people used to sit around in their parlors and play games.
- Explain: Parlor games included Blind Man's Bluff, Pin the Tail on the Donkey, charades, and games of logic.
- Another example is Exquisite Corpse, a parlor game invented by some European artists called the Dadaists at the turn of the 20th century.
- Explain: In Exquisite Corpse, surprises are created by randomly combining words or drawings until the game produces something clever.
- Use this parlor game as inspiration to create a random sentence and use it as a writing prompt.
- Note that Exquisite Corpse has now morphed into an app, which you may want to check out.

Slide 11

- Read this random sentence aloud. (We will go through the steps used to create it in a bit.)
- Ask: What does this mean?
- Confirm that everyone understands these common words.
  - Everyone knows what a toaster is, right?
  - A basement?
  - Dancing?

- Point out that one reason we naturally look for meaning is that this is (in fact) a sentence.

- Remind: Good writing uses structure to help convey meaning.

- Ask: Besides a simple sentence, what other structures can the students list? Especially those having to do with poetry (sonnets, haikus, couplets, etc.).

- Note: Our brains naturally try to make meaning out of patterns—in this case, a sentence.

- Have students pair up and discuss what this sentence could possibly mean. No right or wrong answer, as long as it is logical.

- Focus on coming up with a one- or two-word answer about what the sentence stands for or symbolizes—not a narrative about the toaster. That comes later.

Text Talk

Slide 12: "The Blue Toaster" by Michael Salinger

- Read the poem aloud, have a student read it, and/or play the audio.

Slide 13: "The Blue Toaster" by Sara Holbrook

- Read the poem aloud, have a student read it, and/or play the audio.

Slide 14

- Ask students to turn and talk, comparing the two different poetic interpretations of the random sentence.

- Note that Holbrook changed the sentence to present tense.

- Ask: Which is right? (Of course, neither is right or wrong.)

- Ask: Has each of these poets made some sense out of the random sentence?

- Work backward. Ask students to think about what might have been these poets' one- or two-word interpretation of the sentence before they began writing. Michael: *abandonment*; Sara: *shy*.

Slide 15

- Describe how, in order to try to make sense out of a random sentence, we first examine the pattern of the sentence.

- Refresh students' memories on any parts of speech they might be confused by.

- Make this part quick and painless.

Work Together

Slide 16

- Allot each student six slips of paper (torn-up recycled paper, index cards, sticky notes, etc.).
- Ask students to write down one of each of these word types on a slip of paper, one word per slip.
- Participate along with the students so that in the end there are enough slips to go around.
- Have students place their slips of paper into six stacks. One stack for each part of speech. (All nouns in this stack, all verbs in this stack . . . like that.)
- Create a sentence using one word from each stack.
- Write the sentence on a separate surface.
- See the next slide for some examples of what your sentence will look like.

Slide 17

- Use this as the pattern for your sentence.
- See the next slide for some examples of random sentences.

Slide 18

- Have the students turn and talk about possible meanings for the sentence you have created.
- Remember, we are looking for concepts, not a full-blown narrative yet. Just one- or two-word analyses.
- Note: These analyses will inform your poem as one of them will become the theme for your poem.
- Choose one of these concepts to develop a theme for your group poem.
- Refer back to Slide 14 to see how one sentence produced two different themes.
- Choose a theme for your poem.
- Ask students to turn and talk about possible lines or phrases to add to the poem to develop your chosen theme.
- Remember, poetry doesn't have to be written in complete sentences.
- Ask students to offer lines as they come up with them.
- Write about five to six lines together, which will produce a model for students to follow in their own writing.

Time to Write

Slide 19

- Have each student draw one word from each stack of paper.
- Have them return to their desks and arrange the slips of paper so that they can create a random sentence (next slide).

Slide 20

- Have students get out their writer's notebooks, laptops, or a piece of paper.
- Have the students arrange their words into sentences using this slide as a model.
- Tell them this sentence will become the first line and prompt for their own poems.
- Note that once the sentences are created, the students may rearrange the words and phrase to suit their own creative purposes.
- Be aware that they may wish to change the tense of the sentence.
- Note: Writers may want to make a change for subject/verb agreement.
- Have them write for 7–10 minutes.
- Ignore protests of how random the sentences turn out!
- Remember: This is all part of our scheme to get them to think deeply through making uncommon connections.

Share

Slide 21

- Have students read their poems aloud, all at the same time. Seat symphony!
- Have writers share their work with the students around them.
- Ask for enthusiastic volunteers to read for the class.
- If no one volunteers, ask students to nominate a reader whose work they heard and enjoyed.

Slide 22

- Reiterate that writers use figurative language and uncommon comparisons to connect with their readers.
- Reminder: Writers use patterns to help clarify these connections.
- A surprising comparison is one way to get your audience to stop and think a little bit harder about what they are reading.

Bonus Poems and Lesson Extensions

Slide 23

- These bonus poems have been selected to give you the opportunity to differentiate according to the needs of your classroom and to extend and reinforce the lesson.

Slides 24–25: "Callbacks" by Sara Holbrook

- Read the poem aloud, have a student read it, and/or play the audio.
- Use this opportunity to continue discussions from earlier in the clinic.
- Script this poem for multiple voices and have fun with it.

Slides 26–29: "The Domestique" by Michael Salinger

- Read the poem aloud, have a student read it, and/or play the audio (on Slide 29).
- Give students some background knowledge: A domestique is a cycling team member whose job it is to pull the team's sprinter to the finish line by cutting through the wind before the sprinter.
- Ask: How do comparisons work to strengthen the images in this poem?
- Ask: Are any of these comparisons surprising to you?

Slides 30: "Sticks" by Thomas Sayers Ellis

- Read through just this first excerpt from the poem.
- Ask: What does the poet mean when he describes his father by saying, "His eyes were the worst kind of jury"? (He was judgmental.)
- Ask: What else do we know about his father from this first verse? (He was large and thought being kind was sissified.)

Slide 31

- Finish reading the poem aloud, have a student read it, and/or play the audio.
- Ask: Why did the poet compare himself to a plagiarist? What does a plagiarist do? (Copies others.)
- Ask: What did the poet do to change the direction of his own life? (Through his writing.)
  - Thomas Sayers Ellis, "Sticks" from *The Maverick Room*. Copyright © 2005 by Thomas Sayers Ellis. Reprinted by permission of Graywolf Press. Thomas is an assistant professor of writing at Sarah Lawrence College in New York City. For more information about him, his poetry and publications, please visit www.tsellis.com.

ASSESSMENT

Here we provide a rubric you may choose to use. We provide this as a guide knowing that you may have other goals for your class. Don't feel compelled to assess every skill mentioned in this chart. We have had more success when we zero in on a skill or two with a lesson, but we want to afford you multiple options with these clinics.

Skill	3	2	1
Careful Reading	Demonstrates an understanding of the importance of using comparisons to clarify writing. Knows the difference between simile and metaphor. Is able to articulate meaning beyond the literal.	Partially demonstrates an understanding of the importance of using comparisons to clarify writing. May mistakenly interpret some metaphor literally.	Does not demonstrate an understanding of the importance of using comparisons to clarify writing. Cannot recognize metaphor in text.
Structure and Organization	Demonstrates the ability to recognize and re-create a writing structure that includes metaphorical comparisons. Creates metaphors that are insightful and nuanced.	Partially demonstrates the ability to recognize and re-create a writing structure that includes metaphorical comparisons. Creates some metaphors that may be cliché or illogical.	Does not demonstrate the ability to recognize and re-create a writing structure that includes metaphorical comparisons. Cannot move beyond literal meaning.
Connotative Word Meaning	Demonstrates an understanding of connotative word meanings by making comparisons while using visual language. Metaphors are used creatively and effectively.	Occasionally demonstrates an understanding of connotative word meanings by making comparisons while using visual language. Metaphors don't necessarily clarify the meaning of the piece.	Does not demonstrate an understanding of connotative word meanings by making comparisons while using visual language. Writing is void of metaphor.
Speaking Skills	Consistently demonstrates effective presentation skills using good voice projection, inflection, pacing, eye contact, and stance.	Partially demonstrates effective presentation skills using good voice projection, inflection, pacing, eye contact, and stance.	Does not demonstrate effective presentation skills using good voice projection, inflection, pacing, eye contact, and stance.
Listening Skills	Actively participates in discussions about other students' work and is tuned in to student presentations.	Occasionally participates in discussions about other students' work and is tuned in to student presentations.	Does not participate in discussions about other students' work and is not tuned in to student presentations.

18

The Extended Metaphor

Care and Feeding

WHY TEACH THIS?

Metaphor is the key in the ignition of deeper thinking; it's the wheels spinning across the pavement of communication, the window rolled down through which you shout out your sagest thoughts, the pistons of creativity pounding up and down in the cylinder of a block of text. It's . . .

Okay. You get the drift.

We are often asked, "What is a poem?" or "What is meant by poetical language?" in nonfiction or fiction text. This is it. Reading and picturing a strong metaphor can not only change the way we look at a piece of text, it can change the way we look at the world. After reading Robert Frost, can we ever look at a fork in the road the same way?

This clinic is the third in a series of three on metaphor. We introduced students to the concept of metaphor through another's work in Metaphor Mentor Text (Clinic 16). In Exquisite Metaphors (Clinic 17) we worked on creating metaphor by making uncommon comparisons. In this clinic, we show students how repeated references to a single overarching metaphor helps to ground our writing by linking our text to a single image.

Michael: This is one of my favorite techniques; I've been known to beat a metaphor into submission.

Sara: This is the big one. We have been working on a variety of different writing clinics, many of which point to this goal: demonstrating an understanding of figurative language.

CCSS AND CORRESPONDING ANCHOR STANDARDS

- **Demonstrate** understanding of figurative language, word relationships, and nuances in word meanings.

  [4.L.5] [5.L.5] [6.L.5] [7.L.5] [8.L.5]

- **Interpret** words and phrases as they are used in a text, including determining technical, connotative, and figurative meanings, and analyze how specific word choices shape meaning or tone.

  [4.RL.4] [5.RL.4] [6.RL.4] [7.RL.4] [8.RL.4]

- **Analyze** the structure of texts, including how specific sentences, paragraphs, and larger portions of the text (e.g., a section, a chapter, scene, or stanza) relate to each other and the whole.

  [4.RL.5] [5.RL.5] [6.RL.5] [7.RL.5] [8.RL.5]

- **Read** and comprehend complex literary and informational texts independently and proficiently.

  [4.RL.10] [5.RL.10] [6.RL.10] [7.RL.10] [8.RL.10]

- **Write** informative/explanatory texts to examine and convey complex ideas and information clearly and accurately through the effective selection, organization, and analysis of content.

  [4.W.2] [5.W.2] [6.W.2] [7.W.2] [8.W.2]

- **Write** narrative to develop real or imagined experiences or events using effective technique, well-chosen details, and well-structured sequences.

  [4.W.3] [5.W.3] [6.W.3] [7.W.3] [8.W.3]

- **Produce** clear and coherent writing in which the development, organization, and style are appropriate to task, purpose, and audience.

  [4.W.4] [5.W.4] [6.W.4] [7.W.4] [8.W.4]

- **Demonstrate** command of the conventions of Standard English grammar and usage when writing or speaking.

  [4.L.1] [5.L.1] [6.L.1] [7.L.1] [8.L.1]

PRIOR TO THE LESSON

- Read through the entire lesson and review the slideshow to familiarize yourself with the clinic.

- Note that one of the bonus poems at the end of this clinic may be better suited to use as a model for your class than the one embedded in the clinic. Select the poem that works best for you and your students—your choice.

- Set up a separate surface (chart paper or white board) on which to compose a poem written collectively by you and your students.

- It is most helpful to have completed the other comparison-specific lessons—Simile for Me (Clinic 15), Metaphor Mentor Text (Clinic 16), and Exquisite Metaphors (Clinic 17)—before completing this clinic.

THE LESSON

Slide 1

- Introduce the teaching poets by name (Michael and Sara), as they will appear throughout this lesson.

Slide 2

- Explain: Poetry is personal.
- In this exercise we will write about a personal conflict.

Text Talk

Slides 3–5: "911" by Michael Salinger

- Read the poem aloud, have a student read it, and/or play the audio (Slide 6).

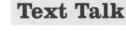
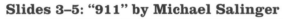

Slide 6

- Ask: Where do you think Michael found the pattern for this piece? (Warning labels on household products—in this case a bottle of bleach, some insecticide, and turpentine.)
- Ask: Does the poem make sense? Why? (Because we are comparing dangerous products to dangerous ideas.)
- Ask: What happens if we substitute a new subject word for the word *hate*?
- Ask: What happens if we were to reword the poem, using the same pattern, and change the word *hate* to *love* or *revenge*? Could the piece still make sense? (Yes, because the extended metaphor is supported by the pattern of the warning labels.)

Work Together

Slide 7

- Brainstorm a list of words about an oncoming thunderstorm on a separate surface.
- *Warning*: This clinic takes up a lot of board space or three sheets of chart paper.
  - You will need sufficient space to build two separate brainstorms and then write a poem together.
  - Start with these questions and add some of your own to create the first brainstorm.

Slide 8

- The white board pictured in this slide is an example of what your list will look like.

- Leave space on your writing surface for a second list, which we will create next.

- Don't spend more than 3 minutes or so on this brainstorm.

- Remember: At this point we want facts, not interpretations.

Slide 9

- Enlist the help of two enthusiastic volunteers to act out an "almost fight."

- Take the two students (actors) aside (in the hallway) for some direction.

- Instruct the two that they will be acting out a real-life scene.

- Explain that they are to go in front of the class and (on cue) brush past one another, and then turn as if they are going to fight.

- *Important*: Tell the two actors that the whole point is that they are trying to capture the moment *before* a fight. They are not to make contact.

- Remind them that they are actors who pretend to overreact to nothing, a mere brush of their shoulders.

- Tell them that after the initial brush, they are to look threatening, hands in fists, glaring. No words, no contact.

- Have them practice the scene once before going before the class.

Slide 10

- Bring your two actors before the class.

- Ask the class to think like reporters.

- Inform them that the two students are going to act out a scene.

- Tell the class to be conscious of what they *do* see and what they *do not* see happen between the two actors.

- Wait until the class is ready, then tell your two actors, "ACTION."

- After their performance, applaud the actors to thank them for being good sports as they return to their seats.

Slide 11

- Make a list of student observations about the almost fight. Record those on the board.

- Use this as your second list—we are still going to need space between the two brainstormed lists to write our poem. (When using markers, we like to make this list in a different color than the list about the thunderstorm.)

- Start with who, what, where.

- Ask:
  - Who was involved? (Two kids.)
  - What happened? (They bumped into each other.)

- What happened to their feet? Did they plant them? Kick a chair? Run away?
- What happened to their hands? Thrown in the air? Made fists?
- How about facial expressions? What happens to a face when it is angry? (Have students try on their angry face.)

- Ask: What did not happen between our two actors? (No punches, no apologies, no hugs, no weapons.)

Slide 12

- Remember, this is just a bullet point list of details.
- Try to steer the students to articulate *how* the actors behaved.
- Remind: We are looking for objective observations, not interpretation or motivation for the actions yet.

Slide 13

- Ask: What do these two events, a thunderstorm and an almost fight, have in common? (Both are conflicts—one in nature one between two people.)
- Ask: Can any of these thunderstorm words be used to describe an almost fight?
- Ask students to turn and talk to come up with a descriptive line about the almost fight using words from the thunderstorm list.

Slide 14

- Craft a poem as a class. Write about the almost fight using the thunderstorm descriptors.
- Remember that it's okay to ask leading questions:
  - How can we describe their hands using the thunderstorm words?
  - What were their eyes doing? Any lightning there?
  - Did they turn like a tornado or did anger swirl between them?
- Leave the poem up as an example for the students to refer to as a mentor text during their time to write.

Slide 15

- Note: By using our thunderstorm words to describe an almost fight, we created an extended metaphor.
- Ask: Does our poem stay true to its original comparison? This is extended metaphor at its most basic level.
- Ask: Do you see how this gives continuity to the poem? Does it make the poem stronger? In what ways? (Ask students to turn and talk.)
- Ask: What do you suppose is meant by a mixed metaphor? (Even if students have never heard this term, they can make inferences.)
- Ask: Why would one extended metaphor be stronger than a mix of metaphors? (Entertain ideas.)

Time to Write

Slide 16

- Announce: Now we will focus on a conflict that is personal to you.
- Note: Our experience is that it is best to craft the pre-write on paper rather than on a computer or tablet.
- Ask students to get out their writer's notebooks or a piece of paper.
- Ask writers to divide the paper in half lengthwise as pictured on the slide.

Slide 17

- Ask writers to think about a time of conflict in their lives.
- Explain that this conflict could be from when they were little, or it could be from 5 minutes ago.
    - It could be a conflict with a person or a thing.
    - A parent, coach, friend, the school bus driver.
    - A computer, a stuck drawer, a zipper on a backpack.
- Expect that some writers will be more willing to take risks with this than others. Some conflicts will be humorous, some deadly serious. Either is okay, but remind students to put themselves in the conflict, to keep it personal. (Not a conflict between your neighbor and his dog, but your conflict listening to them.)
- Remember: Our lesson goal is to create an extended metaphor.
- Note that if they are thinking about an ongoing conflict (such as arguing with parents about chores) they should think about *one specific* time.
- Explain: A poem is a snapshot, not their life story.
- Ask writers to talk it over with a partner before they begin writing.
- Give them a minute or so just to focus on a specific time and start to formulate some recollections.

Slide 18

- Tell students to think like reporters instead of poets.
- Announce: We are going to begin by taking some notes.
- Get the facts down first.
- Walk students through these prompts one at a time.
- Feel free to add some of your own.

Slide 19

- Focus on the setting first.
- Point out that a poem, much the same as a story or a nonfiction descriptive paragraph, has a setting.
- Add specificity. It is doubtful that the writers will use all of the details we are listing, but note taking helps us include more details.
- Walk students through these prompts one at a time.

Slide 20

- Look inside.
- Ask writers to reflect on the actors in the almost fight.
- Ask: Remember what they did with their feet? (Turned and faced off.)
- Ask:
  - What did you do with your feet in your conflict that you are writing about? Stomp away? Run up some stairs?
  - What about your hands?
  - What about your eyes and facial expressions?
  - What happens to you inside when you are working hard *not* to show any reaction, when you are putting on your game face?
  - Where do you carry this kind of tension? Shoulders? Stomach? Jaw? Head?

Slide 21

- Ask writers to draw a thought bubble big enough to contain four to five words.
- Tell them to write down what the conflict felt like inside the bubble.
- Offer this idea: It may help to begin with the words *It was just like . . .*
  - Was it just a little annoying or did it tear them up like a shredding machine?
  - Was it like a tsunami washing over them, a wildfire, a volcano?
  - Was it like a runaway train or a black hole?
- Go around the room and ask writers to say what it was like.
- Respond with something like this: Oh, yours felt like a tornado. Oh, and yours was like a car crash. Good.
- Note: This brief conversation will help students focus on the integral part their metaphor is going to play in the writing of the poem.
- Add a few words related to the conflict in the bubble after writers have identified a metaphorical comparison.
- Example: If the conflict felt like a volcano, related words might be *lava, erupt, fire, mountain.*
- Ask them to make at least one of their related words a verb.

Time to Write

Slide 22

- Ask students to put down their pens or pencils.
- Instruct them to visualize this conflict in their minds.
- Suggest they close their eyes if they are comfortable with that.
- Ask each writer to relive the moment of conflict.

- Allow them 30–45 seconds to do this; it will be a long, quiet 30–45 seconds.
- Instruct the students to visualize the first line in their heads—once they have it, they should open up their folded page and write it down.
- Use the blank half of the folded page for writing the poem. Ask writers to develop their poems with details drawn from their brainstorms.
- Allow 7–10 minutes for the students to draft their poems.
- Remind the writers that they have a whole lot of details at their disposal (in their brainstorm list) and to use as many as possible in their draft.
- Offer reminders as the class is writing, occasionally saying something like:
  - Don't forget to develop your metaphorical comparison.
  - Are you remembering your metaphor?
- As carefully as we have laid the groundwork for this, some students will still forget it in the writing process.

Share

Slide 23

- Reminder: Personal poems can be difficult to share aloud. Some will be humorous, but others are written from a much more tender place.
- Scaffold the sharing process:
  - Ask if a few students would share *in very general terms* the source of their conflict.
  - Ask: Was it a sibling thing? A friend thing? A parent thing? A sports or technology thing?
  - Ask students to read through their poems aloud, everyone reading at the same time. Seat symphony!
- Ask students to read to a partner.
  - Ask the partner to listen for the comparison, the metaphor.
- Ask for a few enthusiastic volunteers to read their poems to the class.

Slide 24

- Reiterate that an extended metaphor is a single comparison that runs through the length of a poem.

Bonus Poems and Lesson Extensions

Slide 25

- These bonus poems have been selected to give you the opportunity to differentiate according to the needs of your classroom and to extend and reinforce the lesson.

Slide 26: "Beef Bone Broth" by Janet S. Wong

- Read the poem aloud, have a student read it, and/or play the audio.
- Ask: How is the poet's grandmother like a pot of boiling broth? (Steaming.)
- Discuss the poet's use of metaphor. (She compares her grandmother, whom we do not know, to the image of a boiling pot of broth, an image we are familiar with.)
- Provide students with some background information about the poet:
  - Janet S. Wong is the author of more than two dozen books for children and teens. She has been honored with the Claremont Stone Center Recognition of Merit, the International Reading Association (IRA) Celebrate Literacy Award, and her appointment to the National Council of Teachers of English poetry award committee and the IRA Notable Books for a Global Society committee. A frequent speaker at schools, libraries, and conferences, Janet Wong has performed at the White House and has been featured on CNN, Fine Living's Radical Sabbatical, and The Oprah Winfrey Show. You can find out more about her at www.janetwong.com.

Slide 27: "The Ordinary" by Ray McNiece

- Read the poem aloud, have a student read it, and/or play the audio.
- Ask: What is the scene of this poem? (A field beside the road.)
- Ask: What might Ray mean by "the red ball"? What could it represent? (Youth, fun, reminiscence.)
- Entertain several options, as there really aren't any right or wrong answers.
- Provide students with some background information about the poet:
  - Ray McNiece is a poet from Cleveland, Ohio. He often performs his poems with his band, Tongue and Groove. This poem comes from his book *Song That Fathoms Home* (Bottom Dog Press, 2003). Find out more about Ray McNiece at www.raymcniece.com.

Slide 28: "Rain Rain Go Away" by Sara Holbrook

- Read the poem aloud, have a student read it, and/or play the audio.
- Point out that this poem looks kind of disorganized on the page.
- Ask: Why do you think Sara did that? (It looks like rain falling and pooling at the bottom of the page.)
- Note: Verb choice is important in this poem.
- Ask: What verbs in the poem describe rain? (*Downpour, dribbles, trickling, pooling.*)
- Note: Verb choice is one way we can sustain a simple metaphor throughout a poem.

ASSESSMENT

Here we provide a rubric you may choose to use. We provide this as a guide knowing that you may have other goals for your class. Don't feel compelled to assess every skill mentioned in this chart. We have had more success when we zero in on a skill or two with a lesson, but we want to afford you multiple options with these clinics.

Skill	3	2	1
Careful Reading	Demonstrates an understanding of the importance of using comparisons to clarify writing. Knows the difference between simile and metaphor. Recognizes extended metaphor and is able to explain why it is appropriate to the subject.	Partially demonstrates an understanding of the importance of using comparisons to clarify writing. May recognize metaphor but cannot discuss how it is extended throughout the text.	Does not demonstrate an understanding of the importance of using comparisons to clarify writing. Cannot recognize extended metaphor in text.
Structure and Organization	Demonstrates the ability to recognize and re-create a writing structure that includes metaphorical comparisons. Uses extended metaphor effectively in the piece.	Partially demonstrates the ability to recognize and re-create a writing structure that includes metaphorical comparisons. May use metaphor but may not extend it throughout the piece or may mix metaphors.	Does not demonstrate the ability to recognize and re-create a writing structure that includes metaphorical comparisons. Cannot move beyond literal meaning.
Connotative Word Meaning	Demonstrates an understanding of connotative word meanings by making comparisons while using visual language. Extended metaphor is used creatively and effectively.	Occasionally demonstrates an understanding of connotative word meanings by making comparisons while using visual language. Metaphors don't necessarily clarify the meaning of the piece or may not be extended throughout the piece.	Does not demonstrate an understanding of connotative word meanings by making comparisons while using visual language. Writing is void of metaphor, extended or otherwise.
Speaking Skills	Consistently demonstrates effective presentation skills using good voice projection, inflection, pacing, eye contact, and stance.	Partially demonstrates effective presentation skills using good voice projection, inflection, pacing, eye contact, and stance.	Does not demonstrate effective presentation skills using good voice projection, inflection, pacing, eye contact, and stance.
Listening Skills	Actively participates in discussions about other students' work and is tuned in to student presentations.	Occasionally participates in discussions about other students' work and is tuned in to student presentations.	Does not participate in discussions about other students' work and is not tuned in to student presentations.

19

Revision Up Close

Self-Edit Checklist

WHY TEACH THIS?

"I love poetry, but I don't know how to assess it."

If we had a nickel for every time we heard this comment—well, we'd have a whole bunch of nickels.

This self-edit checklist is for you and your students to use together when your students are revising the first drafts of their poems. We do not intend for this to be a rubric through which every single piece needs to be strained. Instead, we want you to look at this collection of revision tips as more of a menu—a series of suggested guidelines to be taught and utilized a la carte. We encourage you to take the same approach when assessing your students' work. Don't put too much pressure on every single little poem. Becoming thoughtful, effective writers is a growing process.

No one knows your students' capabilities and challenges better than you do. This is why we chose the clinic approach to presenting the lessons in this book and why we are here offering you and your students these revision considerations—a baker's dozen of them—that mirror the lessons of the clinics. Don't try to address all 13 in one lesson! Instead, selectively draw from them as you work with your students to refine their writing.

In order to properly assess poetry, you will need to define your lesson goals prior to having the students write. Here's a hint: *Today we are going to master the diamante* is not an effective lesson goal. For one thing, to our knowledge, this form does not exist outside of school, which makes us somewhat suspect of it as a stepping stone to literacy. Instead, refer to the "What are we going to learn today" slides that accompany each of our clinics, where we articulate a literacy goal for the lesson. Try using these as models as you develop your own classroom goals for poetry. Assessment then becomes a reflection of the students' ability to meet your goal.

We hope you will use these revision tips in the same way. For instance, you may want to say something like "Today, when we revise our Version 1s, we will want to focus on the details of our writing (#1, Slide 4)." Or you may want to highlight action verbs (#4, Slide 7), and so on. In this way, you can encourage your writers to grow by having them focus on specific skills one at a time and develop a deeper understanding of poetic styles and content knowledge.

As students become familiar with the revision tips here, they will find themselves implementing the strategies as they write—stopping and thinking as they compose. We believe that if students can develop the habit of stopping and thinking, it will serve them well in all of their future communications.

Sara: I think of revision like an escape hatch. It frees me up, knowing that I don't have to get it right the first time.

Michael: Exactly—the most important part of writing is writing. You cannot fix something if it is not there. Revision is what we do after the "typing" part of our writing is done.

CCSS AND CORRESPONDING ANCHOR STANDARDS

- **Demonstrate** understanding of figurative language, word relationships, and nuances in word meanings.

  [4.L.5] [5.L.5] [6.L.5] [7.L.5] [8.L.5]

- **Interpret** words and phrases as they are used in a text, including determining technical, connotative, and figurative meanings, and analyze how specific word choices shape meaning or tone.

  [4.RL.4] [5.RL.4] [6.RL.4] [7.RL.4] [8.RL.4]

- **Analyze** the structure of texts, including how specific sentences, paragraphs, and larger portions of the text (e.g., a section, a chapter, scene, or stanza) relate to each other and the whole.

  [4.RL.5] [5.RL.5] [6.RL.5] [7.RL.5] [8.RL.5]

- **Read** and comprehend complex literary and informational texts independently and proficiently.

  [4.RL.10] [5.RL.10] [6.RL.10] [7.RL.10] [8.RL.10]

- **Write** informative/explanatory texts to examine and convey complex ideas and information clearly and accurately through the effective selection, organization, and analysis of content.

  [4.W.2] [5.W.2] [6.W.2] [7.W.2] [8.W.2]

- **Write** narrative to develop real or imagined experiences or events using effective technique, well-chosen details, and well-structured sequences.

  [4.W.3] [5.W.3] [6.W.3] [7.W.3] [8.W.3]

- **Produce** clear and coherent writing in which the development, organization, and style are appropriate to task, purpose, and audience.

  [4.W.4] [5.W.4] [6.W.4] [7.W.4] [8.W.4]

- **Demonstrate** command of the conventions of Standard English grammar and usage when writing or speaking.

  [4.L.1] [5.L.1] [6.L.1] [7.L.1] [8.L.1]

PRIOR TO THE LESSON

- Print out the checklist found on page 189 of this book.

- Pass out the checklist handout to your students at any point you think is appropriate.

- Decide whether you are going to teach an overview of revision or zero in on a particular revision tip.

THE LESSON

Slide 1

- Don't try to teach all 13 in one lesson! Instead, selectively draw from them as you work with your students refine their writing.

- Introduce the concept that you will be teaching revision as a series of pointers.

- Note that these revision tips can be used with any lesson at any time.

- Remember that the self-edit checklist is for you and your students to use when revising the various drafts of their poems. We do not intend this to be a rubric through which every single piece needs to be strained. Instead, we want you to look at these revision tips as more of a menu—as suggested guidelines to be taught and utilized a la carte. We encourage the same approach when assessing your students' work.

- Understand that no one knows your students' capabilities and challenges better than you do. This is why we chose the clinic approach to presenting the lessons in this book and why we are here offering you and your students these revision considerations—a baker's dozen of them—that mirror the lessons of the clinics.

Slide 2

- Too often students look at revision as a task that is about as pleasant has having their eyes pecked out.

- Ask students to turn and talk about what revision means to them, in writing and in life. (Revision is any time we correct our course to get where we want to go more directly.)

- Ask: What else in life benefits from revision other than writing? Have students turn and talk. (Reframing a question to get a desired answer, adding mustard to a hotdog, changing your batting stance, going back into the house to put on a hat and gloves, etc.)

- Explain to the students that it is better to look at revision as part of the whole writing process, not just extra work that is tacked on to the end.

- Tell students that one of the best things about writing is writers don't have to get it right the first time.
- Remind: We can always go back and revise.
- HOWEVER (big however): We can't revise what is not on the page.
- Draft first and then take the opportunity to improve it.

Slide 3

- Introduce: This clinic includes a baker's dozen of revision tips.
- Decide whether you want to do an overview of all 13 tips or introduce them one at a time. (For further ideas on how to use this clinic, refer to the introduction to Clinic 19 in the book.)
- Don't expect your students to check off every one of these items for every piece of writing.
- Remember, this is an overview of touchstones for thoughtful, accurate communication.
- Introduce these concepts, then consider highlighting or focusing on a subset of these tips when assigning and assessing writing assignments.
- Be aware that the following 13 slides each focus on one aspect of revision.
- Refer back to this exercise multiple times throughout teaching these clinics.

Slide 4

- Have I focused on the details?
  - Poetry is precise.
  - Here, we are looking to strengthen our precision.
  - The piece of writing is focused in time and subject.
  - The details set the scene.
  - Sensory language is used.

Slide 5

- Have I backed up my opinions (subjective terms) with (objective) facts?
  - Review pieces for opinion words.
  - See Clinic 1: Objective Versus Subjective.
  - All opinions should be supported by facts.
  - It is not good enough to say, "The sunset was gorgeous." Better to say, "The sunset was a glowing purple and yellow."
  - Writers may leave the opinion words in their pieces, but only if the subjective terms are supported by evidence.

Slide 6

- Have I chosen the chiefest words?
  - The piece is concise.
  - We discuss the chiefest words in Clinic 3: The Summary Poem.
  - This doesn't simply mean short, but also that the language is rich.

- o Poems don't have to be in complete sentences.
- o Practice eliminating the unnecessary words by circling the most important words.

Slide 7

- Have I used action verbs?
  - o Verbs are our most image-evoking parts of speech.
  - o See Clinic 12: Word Definition Poems and Clinic 13: Weighting the Evidence.
  - o Verbs in the piece create a picture in the reader's mind.
  - o Do the verbs step, sway, prance, and lead the audience to a clearer picture?
  - o Verbs support and/or extend metaphor.

Slide 8

- Have I jettisoned the clichés?
  - o Remind students that if another person can finish any phrase, it is most likely a cliché.
  - o We discuss eliminating clichés in Clinic 10: Personification and Clinic 17: Exquisite Metaphors.
  - o In other words, if I say, "Deer in the . . ." and you guess "headlights," that's a cliché.
  - o The same test works in a Google search. If the search engine is able to guess the phrase, chances are you've got a cliché on your hands.

Slide 9

- Have I written from one pair of shoes?
  - o Unless the poem contains dialogue, it should be written from only one point of view.
  - o We discover point of view and perspective in Clinic 11: Point of View and Clinic 7: No Longer the Same.

Slide 10

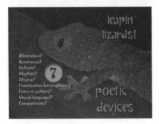

- Have I poeticized my poem?
  - o See Clinic 3: The Summary Poem, Clinic 15: Simile for Me, and Clinics 16–18 (on metaphor).
  - o Poetic devices have been used effectively.
  - o Poetic devices are appropriate to tone and theme.
  - o Poetic devices are not overused.

Slide 11

- Have I maintained a consistent pattern?
  - o Patterns may be broken with purpose for dramatic intent.
  - o See Clinic 6: Couplets on the Brain and Clinic 10: Personification.
  - o The layout of the poem on the page helps convey deeper meaning.

Slide 12

- Is rhyme pushing my poem around?
  - Rhyme has purpose.
  - See Clinic 6: Couplets on the Brain.
  - A poem is not simply a rhyming word group.
  - Rhyme helps the poem convey meaning and is not distracting.

Slide 13

- Did I use one strong comparison to convey my meaning?
  - See Clinic 15: Simile for Me, Clinics 16–18 (on metaphor), and Clinic 7: No Longer the Same.
  - Are my similes and/or metaphors consistent?
  - Comparisons should be universally comprehensible.
  - Are there too many comparisons and do they fight with one another?
  - Simile and metaphor create and clarify meaning through figurative language.

Slide 14

- Have I read my poem aloud? Does it flow smoothly?
  - A poem has a voice, and that should be the natural voice of the speaker.
  - See Clinic 11: Point of View and Clinic 10: Personification.
  - The poem's voice matches the point of view of the speaker (the poet or the persona the poet has assumed).
  - Words such as *whilst* and *wherefore* have no place in a 21st century poem, unless it is written from the perspective of someone from a previous time.
  - If the students are working on their pieces in class, it helps to have them read their work aloud—everyone reading at the same time, a seat symphony.
  - Even shy writers will read aloud in the privacy of a cacophony of voices.
  - Next, ask writers to read aloud to a partner.
  - Encourage students to give honest feedback to their partners, responding with one good comment and one suggestion for improvement.

Slide 15

- Have I double-checked the basics—grammar and spelling?
  - Grammar matters in a final draft.
  - Reading the piece aloud is a good way to catch those "obvious" mistakes.

Slide 16

- Have I shared my poem?
  - A poem is never truly finished until it has been shared and discussed.
  - Opportunities to share poetry are everywhere.
  - Share with a partner, reading aloud. On a blog, a podcast, a PowerPoint, the morning announcements. Take sidewalk chalk and surround the school with poetry. Post poetry in the hallways. Use student poems to begin class, not just poems from the library. Practice inflection by reading the poetry of other students.
  - The more poetry is shared, the more freely it can be discussed with candor.
  - The more poetry is discussed, the more options writers will see for improving their writing.

20

Speaking Out

Public Speaking With Conviction

WHY TEACH THIS?

The number-one fear of mankind is public speaking, according to various and sundry studies. Death came in at third in one of those reports. So accordingly, the comedian Jerry Seinfeld has postulated that, given the choice, we would rather be in the coffin than delivering the eulogy.

While we can't guarantee that we can alleviate all of your students' stage fright, we can provide you with some tips to make their forays into oral presentations a bit more successful. We believe these initial successes will lay the groundwork for helping them become confident speakers who get their messages across with conviction.

The rubric in this lesson will provide your class with a vocabulary that they may use to self-assess and to give peer critiques of their oral presentations.

Michael: I can truly say that no small amount of any success I have had over the years has been due to my ability to look someone in the eye and speak with composure.

Sara: I have repeatedly found that reading my poetry aloud informs not only my audience, but also my own writing. I need to say the words, feel how they flow. For me, reading aloud is an integral part of the revision process.

CCSS AND CORRESPONDING ANCHOR STANDARDS

- **Present** information, findings, and supporting evidence such that listeners can follow the line of reasoning and the organization, development and style are appropriate to the task, purpose, and audience.

  [4.SL.4] [5.SL.4] [6.SL.4] [7.SL.4] [8.SL.4]

- **Adapt** speech to a variety of contexts and communicative tasks, demonstrating command of formal English when indicated or appropriate.

  [4.SL.6] [5.SL.6] [6.SL.6] [7.SL.6] [8.SL.6]

PRIOR TO THE LESSON

- Read through the entire lesson and review the slideshow to familiarize yourself with the clinic.

- Make sure students have in front of them a piece they have written or an example text you have selected that they may mark up and use to practice these techniques aloud.

THE LESSON

Slide 1

- Introduce the lesson. This lesson is about public speaking.

- Don't have everyone reading the same text or it will become an exercise in choral reading. Follow along with the Tasmanian Devil.

Slide 2

- Explain that public speaking is no doubt the first form of mass communication.

- Ask students to turn and talk about occasions when public speaking is a necessity.

- Note: Even though it is considered one of people's major fears, it is a skill that will serve people well no matter what they decide to do with their lives.

Slide 3

- Ask students to list habits and mistakes people might make when speaking to an audience that may keep them from being understood.

- Give examples:
  - Playing with your hair
  - Swaying back and forth
  - Speaking too quietly
  - Looking down at the ground

Slide 4

- Explain: We are going to break down the strategies for good public speaking into five components.

- Note that our goal is to be able to deliver a speech in front of an audience in a convincing, confident, and understandable manner.

- Explain: We are not concerned with grand dramatization or character as much as the competent delivery of a text. (Drama could be the next step as we hone our skills even further.)

Slide 5

- PIPES is the acronym we will use to help us with public speaking.

- Offer a reminder of the definition of acronym (**P**rojection, **I**nflection, **P**acing, **E**ye contact, **S**tance).

- Announce: We will go over each of these items on the following slides one by one.

Slide 6: Projection

- Explain that there is a difference between projecting and yelling.

- Yelling distorts the voice and hurts our throat as well as the audience's ears.

- Illustrate this point with a clear example: In the same way a slide projector makes an image bigger without distorting the image, speakers must project their voices to the point where they are loud enough to be heard by the most distant listener but clear enough to be understood by the entire audience.

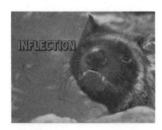

Slide 7

- Ask students to read the texts they have in front of them aloud—everyone at the same time.

- Start them out just sitting at their desks.

- Instruct the students to be loud enough to hear themselves over their neighbors without yelling.

- Walk around the class speaking out loud yourself, and encourage the students to match your volume as you pass them.

- Explain to the students that the volume they are using in this mish-mash chorus is very near the volume they will need when presenting their pieces solo.

- Working in a group like this provides a reference point for the participants to refer to later.

- Reiterate that projection is not yelling.

Slide 8: Inflection

- Define inflection as the emotion and emphasis we put on our spoken words.

- Explain that when we are told to read with more emotion or feeling, inflection is what is being requested.

- Tell students that inflection includes dynamics—speaking more loudly and more quietly as the text infers (while still making sure one is heard by the whole audience).

Slide 9

- Read through these excerpts.

- Have students pair up to read to one another.

- Notice how the language and rhythm of the lines require different styles of inflection.

- Choose a couple of lines from one of the pieces and read through them a few times, emphasizing different words each time.
- Ask: How do the different emphases color the way the line might be interpreted?
- Ask: What is the difference in a speaker's inflection when they ask a question, state a fact, or are trying to persuade?

Slide 10: Pacing

- Ask: What is meant by *pacing*?
- Note: It is not walking back and forth like our devilish friend above.
- Explain: We are speaking about the speed with which people speak their words.
- Let students know that a good rule of thumb is that the larger the audience, the slower the pace and more frequent the pauses.

Slide 11

- Read through this piece aloud with your students.
- Notice how the phrase *shrilly sung crescendos* requires a reader to slow down a bit because of its tongue-twister characteristics.
- Have students ask themselves, "Am I able to articulate the text at the speed I am speaking?"
- Instruct students to read the pieces they have in front of them out loud— first as fast as they can, then again in slow motion, then again at what they consider the perfect speed for an audience the size of the class.
- Note that not only will the students be practicing their pacing, they will be doing repeated readings of their text, also known as rehearsing.

Slide 12: Eye Contact

- Simply put—look at your audience.
- Explain that pacing and pausing help a reader take the time to look up at the audience.
- Reminder: Rehearsal helps!
- Demonstrate that tricks like looking over the audience's heads to fake eye contact won't work—it will be noticeable.

Slide 13

- Give students these tricks to help with making eye contact:
- Treat the page you are holding as if it were a plate on which the words are resting. It is not a mirror to hold in front of your face.
- Use your thumb to keep your place as you look up from the page to make eye contact with your audience.

- Make sure the font size of your text is large enough to facilitate easy reading.
- Memorize the first line or so of the piece and be sure to deliver this looking at your audience. The first and last lines are the most important to make eye contact on.

Slide 14: Stance

- Explain that *stance* refers to anything one is doing with their body in front of their audience.
- Refer back to your earlier discussion about distracting things the students have seen public speakers do.
- Note that in the introduction to public speaking, it is most important to cut out distracting movement.
- Instruct the students to stand with a good base—feet shoulder width apart like our Tasmanian friend above.
- Tell students not to lock their knees; they are the body's shock absorbers.
- Remind them: No swaying, pulling at clothes, snapping fingers, knee shaking, hair eating, eye rolling, incessant blinking, etc.

Slide 15

- Here are Michael and Sara in action.
- Ask: Even without hearing their voices, what can you infer from these pictures?
- Bring a student to the front of the class and have them read their piece for the rest of the room.
- Using PIPES as a rubric, critique the speaker's performance.
- Ask: Which of these five things did our speaker do best?
- Then ask: If you had to pick just one of the remaining attributes for improvement, which would it be?
- Explain that this is how they may use PIPES as a tool to self-assess their work with each other.
- Emphasize the importance of always letting the speaker know what they are doing best and then what points they need to improve on the most.
- Run through this exercise with a few more students and then have the class work with partners and coach one another.
- Don't try to improve more than one skill at a time. It is too confusing to try to improve more than one component of PIPES at a time. As a speaker gets better at their weakest skill, it becomes easier to work on improving the next skill.
- Explain: No matter how proficient a speaker is, there is always one of these attributes they can improve on. And no matter how inexperienced a speaker is, they are better at one of these than the others.

Slide 16

- Use your PIPES!

Bonus Poems and Lesson Extensions

Slide 17

- These bonus poems have been selected to give you the opportunity to differentiate according to the needs of your classroom and to extend and reinforce the lesson.

Slide 18: "Appearances to the Contrary" by Sara Holbrook

- Have some fun with this one!
- Choose five enthusiastic volunteers to come to the front of the class.
- Have each student read one line of the poem while acting it out.
- At the end, have them all repeat their motions with the last line. (*Why do you treat me like a kid?*)

Slide 19: "The Poetry Instructor" by Michael Salinger

- Note: Teachers and fellow poetry instructors, we put this sonnet in here for you!

ASSESSMENT

Here we provide a rubric you may choose to use. We provide this as a guide knowing that you may have other goals for your class. Don't feel compelled to assess every skill mentioned in this chart. We have had more success when we zero in on a skill or two with a lesson, but we want to afford you multiple options with these clinics.

Skill	3	2	1
Projection	Demonstrates the ability to speak with proper projection for the audience. Is not too loud, nor too soft. All words are heard by all audience members.	Partially demonstrates the ability to speak with proper projection for the audience. May trail off at the end of lines or may be too loud once or twice during recitation.	Is either too quiet to be heard or too loud to be understood.
Inflection	Demonstrates the ability to use pitch and dynamics in a way that enhances the audience's understanding of the text being spoken.	Partially demonstrates the ability to use pitch and dynamics while reciting a piece. May fall into a sing-song or inappropriately overemphasize a word.	Does not demonstrate the ability to use pitch and dynamics while reciting a piece. Reading is monotone or full of inappropriately or overemphasized words.
Pacing	Demonstrates the ability to control pace, using pauses effectively and articulating all words to enhance the audience's understanding of the text being spoken.	Partially demonstrates the ability to control pacing, pauses, and articulation. May perform portions of text either too fast or too slow. May miss an opportunity to use a pause for dramatic effect.	Is unable to demonstrate the ability to control pacing, pauses, or articulation. Speed reads through text or loses place several times when reading from the page.
Eye Contact	Demonstrates the ability to make eye contact across the whole audience and to create a feeling of conversation with listeners.	Occasionally demonstrates the ability to make eye contact with the audience. May only occasionally look up from text.	Does not demonstrate the ability to make eye contact with audience. Never looks up from the page, or stares off into space.
Stance	Consistently demonstrates effective stance. Does not display any distracting movements and adds to the audience's understanding of the piece by using appropriate body language.	Partially demonstrates effective stance. May display a distracting or cliché movement or two.	Does not demonstrate effective stance. Movements during recitation are distracting or disconnected from text being spoken.

Revision Checklist

☐ **1. Have I focused on the details?** A poem is a snapshot; it is not a whole movie. My poem should clearly capture a moment in time. Did I describe the place, the time, the event through detailed imagery, including one or more of my senses? Is there a place where I can strengthen my word picture?

☐ **2. Have I backed up my opinions (subjective terms) with (objective) facts?** Words such as *good* and *bad*, *fabulous* and *terrible* all need to be supported by objective facts and details. It is not enough to say the flowers were pretty, dumb, or weird.

☐ **3. Have I chosen the chiefest words?** Poets are stingy with words. Have I used powerful words and eliminated words that I don't need? Are there more words I could lose?

☐ **4. Have I used action verbs?** Does my poem move out? I don't want to say "It came into view in a lively manner" if I can say "It swung into view." Is there a place where I can strengthen my verbs?

☐ **5. Have I jettisoned the clichés?** Phrases such as *deer in the headlights*, *screamed like a banshee*, and *black as night* are annoying enough when Mom uses them. They are even worse in our writing. Can I reword any overused phrases?

☐ **6. Have I written from one pair of shoes?** Often first drafts appear to be speaking from more than one perspective, perhaps beginning in first person, switching midstream to second person, and ending up in some philosophical third person summary (*I hate anchovies, anchovies make you sick, anchovies are stinko*). Unless the poem contains dialogue, it has only one point of view.

☐ **7. Have I double-checked the basics?** Subject-verb agreement? Present, future, or past tense (choose one)? Spell checked? Readable font or handwriting? Grammar mistakes can get in the way of my audience's understanding. Have I eliminated them?

☐ **8. Have I poeticized my poem?** Are the poetic devices appropriate to the tone and theme of my poem? Have I overused any of these devices? Have I used poetic devices effectively?

☐ **9. Have I maintained a consistent pattern?** Poetry may put details in a pattern (couplets, sonnets, haiku, shape, or one I've made up). If I used a pattern, is it consistent? If I broke a pattern, was it on purpose? Have I used my patterns purposefully?

☐ **10. Is rhyme pushing my poem around?** Rhyme can be fun and effective, but I don't want it to be driving my poem off a cliff into a silly pit of nonsense. Does the rhyme help my poem or hurt it? Can I rearrange or reword my poem to get rid of forced, fake, or too predictable rhymes?

☐ **11. Did I use strong comparison(s) to clarify my meaning?** Did I use simile or metaphor to help my audience see and understand what I am saying? Are there too many comparisons and do they fight with one another? Can I sharpen my comparisons?

☐ **12. Does the poem flow smoothly?** In reading my poem aloud, does it sound natural? Am I using a believable voice, whether I am speaking for myself or from another pair of shoes? Is my vocabulary appropriate to my subject and voice? Is there a place where I can make the voice of my poem sound more natural?

☐ **13. Have I shared my poem?** Does it make sense if I don't explain it? If my audience is confused about my message, have I listened to their concerns and made changes? A confusing poem is an unfinished poem.

About the Poets

Susan Campbell Bartolleti is an award-winning author of nonfiction books. She also writes poetry from her backyard snuggery in Scranton, Pennsylvania. For more information about Susan and her dynamic career, please visit www.scbartoletti.com.

Larry Dane Brimner is a dog lover who has written a lot of books—big books, little books, and in-between books. Always fun and full of facts, he is the recipient of numerous awards for his writing of nonfiction. You can find out more about Larry, his books, school visits, and teacher workshops at www.brimner.com.

Lucille Clifton moves her readers through direct language and real-world situations. Her honors include an Emmy Award from the American Academy of Television Arts and Sciences, a Lannan Literary Award, two fellowships from the National Endowment for the Arts, the Shelley Memorial Award, the YM-YWHA Poetry Center Discovery Award, and the Ruth Lilly Prize, in addition to two of her books being nominated for Pulitzer Prizes. If you are not acquainted with her, find out more at www.poets.org/poet.php/prmPID/79.

Emily Dickinson (1830–1886) was an American poet. She is regarded as one of America's greatest poets, but she is also well known for being a bit of a hermit. Living a life of simplicity and seclusion, she wrote poetry of great power. Her use of short, compact phrases set her work apart from other poets writing in her time.

Rebecca Kai Dotlich writes poetry and picture books. From *Lemonade Sun* to *Rumbling Riddles*, you can find more out about Rebecca, her books, and her school visits by visiting www.rebeccakaidotlich.com.

Sharon Draper is a *New York Times* best-selling children's and young adult author, a former teacher and teacher of the year. She is the recipient of numerous awards for her writing. For more information about Sharon and her stellar books, visit www.sharondraper.com.

Paul Laurence Dunbar (1872–1906) grew up in Dayton, Ohio, where he was a classmate of the Wright Brothers. He was the first African American poet to come to prominence before dying of tuberculosis at the age of 33. For more information, visit www.dunbarsite.org.

Thomas Sayers Ellis is an assistant professor of writing at Sarah Lawrence College in New York City. For more information about him, his poetry and publications, please visit www.tsellis.com.

Robert Frost was an American poet. He was the winner of four Pulitzer Prizes, writing mainly about rural life in New England. For more information about him, visit www.poets.org/poet.php/prmPID/192.

Nikki Grimes is an award-winning poet and author and the winner of the National Council of Teachers of English Excellence in Children's Poetry Award. She lives in California and is also a talented artist and photographer. You can find out more information about her at www.nikkigrimes.com.

Kelly Harris-DeBerry lives and writes in New Orleans, Louisiana, where she is the creator of Poems & Pink Ribbons, a poetry workshop for breast cancer patients, survivors, and their loved ones. She holds a Master of Fine Arts from Lesley University and is widely published. You can find out more about her at www.kellyharrispoetry.com.

David Harrison is the author of more than 80 books for kids and adults. For more information about David and his lively books, please visit www.davidlharrison.com. While you are there, be sure to click on the link to his blog, which is full of classroom ideas and poetry.

Georgia Heard is an esteemed poet, author, and educator who lives in Florida and travels the world speaking about and through poetry. More information about Georgia can be found at www.georgiaheard.com. *The Arrow Finds Its Mark* (Roaring Brook Press, 2012) is a rich resource for found poems.

Paul Janeczko is a former teacher and an esteemed poet. For poems he has written in the voices of others, check out his book *Requiem: Poems of the Terezin Ghetto* (Candlewick Press), and for more ideas about the reading of poetry, *Reading Poetry* (Heinemann). These are just two of his many titles; you can find out more information, including about school visits, by visiting www. paulbjaneczko.com.

Ben Johnson was a contemporary of William Shakespeare, an English Renaissance dramatist, poet, and actor active in the 17th century English literary scene.

J. Patrick Lewis is a former U.S. Children's Poet Laureate and the winner of the National Council of Teachers of English Excellence in Children's Poetry Award. His books are both fun and chock full of all kinds of information. Please check out his website at http://jpatricklewis.com.

Charles Mackay (1814–1888) was a Scottish poet, journalist, author, anthologist, novelist, and songwriter who wrote and philosophized about society.

Marie-Elizabeth Mali is the author of *Steady, My Gaze* (Tebot Bach, 2011) and co-editor with Annie Finch of the anthology *Villanelles* (Everyman's Library Pocket Poets, 2012). She is an avid underwater photographer. When Marie-Elizabeth is not traveling the globe in search of sea images, she resides in New York City. For more information please visit www.memali.com.

Ray McNiece is a poet from Cleveland, Ohio. He often performs his poems with his band, Tongue and Groove. Find out more about Ray McNiece at www.raymcniece.com.

Christina Rossetti was born and raised in London; however, her parents were Italian. She was quite famous in her time. Find more information at www.poetryfoundation.org/bio/christina-rossetti.

Pam Muñoz Ryan is mostly known for her award-winning picture books and novels. Like many writers, she also appreciates and writes poetry. You can learn more about her at www.pammunozryan.com.

John Godfrey Saxe (1816–1867) was an American poet from Vermont, a journalist and satirist who is best remembered for introducing the Indian fable of the blind men and the elephant to western audiences.

Steve Swinburne is the author of many nonfiction books for kids, a zombie aficionado, and a ukulele maestro. Learn more about Steve, his books, and his rollicking school visits at www.steveswinburne.com.

Elizabeth Thomas is a teaching poet who divides her time between homes in Connecticut and Florida. Elizabeth is widely published and is a coach of the CT Brave New Voices Teen Poetry Slam team. You can read more about her at www.upwordspoetry.com/EBio.htm.

Lao Tzu (one of a variety of spellings in use), loosely translated as "old master," was a Chinese poet, philosopher, scholar, and teacher from the 6th century BCE, or perhaps the 4th or 5th century. No one really knows. The endurance of his words is what matters most, and you can find out more about him online.

Amy Ludwig VanDerwater is a writer and teacher living on Heart Rock Farm (The Poem Farm) in Holland, New York. For more information about her, please visit www.poemfarm.amylv.com.

Walt Whitman (1819–1892) was an American poet and journalist. His major work was *Leaves of Grass*, which he self-published in 1855. He is probably the most famous of all American poets. For more information, visit www.poets.org/poet.php/prmPID/126.

William Carlos Williams (1883–1963) was a poet and a physician, part of what was called the Imagist movement. He experimented with creating strong images that capture a moment in time. You can find out more about Williams at www.poets.org/poet.php/prmPID/119.

John Greenleaf Whittier (1807–1892) was from Massachusetts, a Quaker who devoted his life and talents to the abolitionist movement for more than 20 years. He was a performance poet, renting halls to give poetry readings and reading on street corners, trying to direct the attention of the public to the abolitionist movement. For more information about Whittier, visit www.johngreenleafwhittier.com.

Allan Wolf is an award-winning poet and performer. A delightful, insightful writer and presenter, he hails from North Carolina. You can get to know about him, his books, and his "po-shows" by visiting www.allanwolf.com.

Janet S. Wong is the author of more than two dozen books for children and teens. She has been honored with the Claremont Stone Center Recognition of Merit, the International Reading Association (IRA) Celebrate Literacy Award, and her appointment to the National Council of Teachers of English poetry award committee and the IRA Notable Books for a Global Society committee. A frequent speaker at schools, libraries, and conferences, she has performed at the White House and has been featured on CNN, Fine Living's Radical Sabbatical, and The Oprah Winfrey Show. Visit her website at www.janetwong.com.

Jane Yolen has been called the Hans Christian Andersen of America and the Aesop of the 20th century. She has written more than 300 books; won numerous awards for her poetry, picture books, and novels; and is the recipient of six honorary doctorates in literature. It's hard to keep up with her, but you can find out more about her accomplishments and writing at www.janeyolen.com.

Index of Poems

By Clinic Number

Clinic	Slide	Title	Author	First Line
12	24	Novice	Salinger, Michael	Novice hasn't quite figured things out yet
12	25	Tao Te Ching, #11	Lao Tzu	Thirty spokes share the wheel's hub
13	4	100% Me	Holbrook, Sara	10% giggles
13	17	Mountain Bike Soufflé	Salinger, Michael	Take a good-sized bowl,
13	26	Labels	Holbrook, Sara	People get tagged
13	27	Recipe for Unity	Harris, Kelly	Start honest.
13	28	Recipe for Genocide	Holbrook, Sara	In a caldron of instability
14	13	Love Heals	Holbrook, Sara	Across oceans, miles, the street
14	14	Five-Paragraph Essay	Salinger, Michael	After the games are finished
14	22	About My MVP Award	Wolf, Allan	Despite an entire season on the bench
15	9	A Simile of Me	Holbrook, Sara	Stubborn as a dandelion
15	15	Flint	Rossetti, Christina	An emerald is as green as grass,
15	16	Like Me or Knot	Grimes, Nikki	I kiss your neck like a whisper,
15	18	The Longest Home Run	Lewis, J. Patrick	Mickey Mantle
15	19	A Poem Is …	Salinger, Michael	A poem is like Kool-Aid
16	13	Disappointment	Holbrook, Sara	Disappointment!
16	19	Topography of Me	Holbrook, Sara	The landscape of my arm
16	26	Divided	Holbrook, Sara	We're not a unit anymore.
16	28	He Had His Dream	Dunbar, Paul Laurence	He had his dream, and all through his life,
16	30–31	Belay Off	Salinger, Michael	Belay off.
17	12	The Blue Toaster	Salinger, Michael	The frightened
17	13	The Blue Toaster	Holbrook, Sara	The frightened blue toaster
17	24–25	Callbacks	Holbrook, Sara	Okay.
17	27–29	Domestique	Salinger, Michael	Muscle fatigue is instigated
17	30–31	Sticks	Ellis, Thomas Sayers	My father was an enormous man
18	6	911	Salinger, Michael	Hate is extremely flammable
18	26	Beef Bone Broth	Wong, Janet S.	This bowl of beef bone broth
18	27	The Ordinary	McNiece, Ray	Some days the sky is merely
18	28	Rain, Rain, Go Away	Holbrook, Sara	No
19	19	The Poetry Instructor	Salinger, Michael	They look at me and ask "What should I write?"
20	11	Turning Back	Holbrook, Sara	October light
20	18	Appearances to the Contrary	Holbrook, Sara	I grip my fists

By Author

Author	Clinic	Slide	Title	First Line
Holbrook, Sara	12	9	Subtle	Subtle
Holbrook, Sara	12	21	Love	I've noticed there's a
Holbrook, Sara	12	23	Democracy	Not a flagpole, pointing heavenward
Holbrook, Sara	13	4	100% Me	10% giggles
Holbrook, Sara	13	26	Labels	People get tagged
Holbrook, Sara	13	28	Recipe for Genocide	In a caldron of instability
Holbrook, Sara	14	13	Love Heals	Across oceans, miles, the street
Holbrook, Sara	15	9	A Simile of Me	Stubborn as a dandelion
Holbrook, Sara	16	13	Disappointment	Disappointment!
Holbrook, Sara	16	19	Topography of Me	The landscape of my arm
Holbrook, Sara	16	26	Divided	We're not a unit anymore.
Holbrook, Sara	17	13	The Blue Toaster	The frightened blue toaster
Holbrook, Sara	17	24–25	Callbacks	Okay.
Holbrook, Sara	18	28	Rain, Rain, Go Away	No
Holbrook, Sara	20	11	Turning Back	October light
Holbrook, Sara	20	18	Appearances to the Contrary	I grip my fists
Janeczko, Paul	11	17	Mary Todd Lincoln Speaks of Her Son's Death, 1862	When Willie died of the fever
Johnson, Ben	12	22	It Was a Beauty That I Saw	A skein of silk
Lao Tzu	12	25	Tao Te Ching, #11	Thirty spokes share the wheel's hub
Lewis, J. Patrick	15	18	The Longest Home Run	Mickey Mantle
Mackay, Charles	10	39	The Children's Auction	Who bids for the little children—
Mali, Marie-Elizabeth	2	25	In the Deep	Coral in the shapes of brains, fans,
McNiece, Ray	18	27	The Ordinary	Some days the sky is merely
Rossetti, Christina	15	15	Flint	An emerald is as green as grass,
Ryan, Pam Muñoz	10	38	Line Breaks	Never separate
Salinger, Michael	1	29	Gruesome	Gruesome is kind of hard to look at
Salinger, Michael	2	10	Two Wheels That Go Around	Two wheels that go around
Salinger, Michael	3	38–39	Don't You Boys Know Any Nice Songs?	the drummer's playing ultra-loud
Salinger, Michael	4	11	Hardware Store	All purpose
Salinger, Michael	4	30	Digestion	We have a mouth where the food goes in.
Salinger, Michael	5	27	Hungry	I am
Salinger, Michael	6	29	Martin Luther King	Martin Luther King had an American Dream.

By First Line of Poem

First Line	Clinic	Slide	Title	Author
The guinea pig has fleas,	9	12	It's All My Fault	Holbrook, Sara
The landscape of my arm	16	19	Topography of Me	Holbrook, Sara
The world below the brine,	2	6	The World Below the Brine	Whitman, Walt
They look at me and ask "What should I write?"	19	19	The Poetry Instructor	Salinger, Michael
Thirty spokes share the wheel's hub	12	25	Tao Te Ching, #11	Lao Tzu
This bowl of beef bone broth	18	26	Beef Bone Broth	Wong, Janet S.
Transience	7	22	Transience	Holbrook, Sara
Twinkle, twinkle, little bat	6	28	Untitled	Carroll, Lewis
Twinkle, twinkle, little star	6	27	The Star	Taylor, Jane
Two wheels that go around	2	10	Two Wheels That Go Around	Salinger, Michael
We have a mouth where the food goes in.	4	30	Digestion	Salinger, Michael
We're not a unit anymore.	16	26	Divided	Holbrook, Sara
What's the purpose	8	5	What's the Point?	Holbrook, Sara
When	10	36	Do They Know?	VanDerwater, Amy Ludwig
When Willie died of the fever	11	17	Mary Todd Lincoln Speaks of Her Son's Death, 1862	Janeczko, Paul
Where does the sky begin?	8	16	Where Does the Sky Begin?	Salinger, Michael
Who bids for the little children—	10	39	The Children's Auction	Mackay, Charles
Wood pusher.	2	21	Skater	Holbrook, Sara
Yarp. Arp. Arp. Arp. Arp.	4	28	Weekday Morning Haiku	Holbrook, Sara
Yes	1	32	My Official List	Holbrook, Sara
You are not the boss of me	5	28	Feelings Make Me Real	Holbrook, Sara
You could say Jinx is loaded with luck	12	8	Jinx	Salinger, Michael
You think the sun spots are more bright?	9	28	Dog Daze	Holbrook, Sara

CORWIN
A SAGE Company

The Corwin logo—a raven striding across an open book—represents the union of courage and learning. Corwin is committed to improving education for all learners by publishing books and other professional development resources for those serving the field of PreK–12 education. By providing practical, hands-on materials, Corwin continues to carry out the promise of its motto: **"Helping Educators Do Their Work Better."**

About the Authors

Sara Holbrook is a full-time educator, author/poet, and consultant who has been teaching in classrooms across the United States and abroad for more than twenty years. She is the author of over a dozen books for children, adults, and teachers, as well as an award-winning performance poet. A frequent keynote speaker, Sara shows teachers how to use writing and oral presentation exercises to help raise vocabulary and other literacy skills, along with how to improve teacher comprehension through collaboration, writing, and classroom performance across all grade levels and content areas.

A fixture in the performance poetry and education community, **Michael Salinger** has been writing and performing poetry and fiction for more than twenty years. His work has appeared in dozens of literary journals published in the United States and Canada, and he has coauthored two professional books with Sara: *Outspoken!* and *High-Definition*. Michael is also the founder and chief facilitator of the teen writing and performance program at Cleveland's Playhouse Square Foundation—the second largest performing arts center in the United States after Broadway.